THE KNIGHT'S TALE

FROM THE CANTERBURY TALES
BY

GEOFFREY CHAUCER

*Edited with an Introduction, Notes
and Glossary by*

A. C. SPEARING

*The right of the
University of Cambridge
to print and sell
all manner of books
was granted by
Henry VIII in 1534.
The University has printed
and published continuously
since 1584.*

CAMBRIDGE UNIVERSITY PRESS

CAMBRIDGE

LONDON   NEW YORK   NEW ROCHELLE

D0345631

Published by the Press Syndicate of the University of Cambridge
The Pitt Building, Trumpington Street, Cambridge CB2 1RP
32 East 57th Street, New York, NY 10022, USA
10 Stamford Road, Oakleigh, Melbourne 3166, Australia

Library of Congress catalogue card number: 66–13641

ISBN 0 521 04633 5

First published 1966
Thirteenth printing 1985

Printed in Great Britain at the
University Press, Cambridge

CONTENTS

ACKNOWLEDGEMENTS

This edition could not have been prepared without help of various kinds. *The Knight's Tale* has been much written about in this century, often at an extremely high level of criticism and scholarship. In addition to the 'Suggestions for Further Reading' listed on p. 190, I have found the following particularly helpful: W. C. Curry, *Chaucer and the Mediaeval Sciences* (Allen and Unwin, 1960); William Frost, 'An Interpretation of Chaucer's *Knight's Tale*', *Review of English Studies* (1949); J. Seznec, *The Survival of the Pagan Gods* (Pantheon, New York, 1953); Dale Underwood, 'The First of the *Canterbury Tales*', *E.L.H.* (1959). In writing about the customs of medieval war in my Introduction, I have plundered without detailed acknowledgement from Stuart Robertson, 'Elements of Realism in the *Knight's Tale*', *Journal of English and Germanic Philology* (1915), and M. H. Keen, *The Law of War in the Later Middle Ages* (Routledge and Kegan Paul, 1965). I am also, of course, much indebted to earlier editions of *The Knight's Tale*, and particularly to that of Professor J. A. W. Bennett (Harrap, 2nd ed., revised 1958).

My greatest debt is to my wife. The notes and glossary of this edition have been composed in collaboration with her, and she has revised and elucidated the Introduction. She has also prepared a large proportion of the typescript, and has generally made the whole task far easier and more pleasant than it would otherwise have been. Any errors are of course my own responsibility.

A. C. S.

Cambridge
October 1965

INTRODUCTION

Like most of Chaucer's poetry, and indeed like most medieval literature, *The Knight's Tale* is not original in its story. It was not the habit of medieval writers to invent their own stories; on the contrary, they were pleased to be able to claim the authority of age for the tales they told, and to begin

> Whilom, as olde stories tellen us....

The Knight's Tale is unquestionably derived from a specific written source, though Chaucer does not anywhere say what it is. It is in fact the *Teseida* of Giovanni Boccaccio, an Italian poet of Chaucer's own time, from whose work he translated the whole or part of a number of his own poems. Notably, Chaucer's longest single work, *Troilus and Criseyde*, is essentially a translation of Boccaccio's *Filostrato*, while Chaucer borrows from the *Teseida* not only in *The Knight's Tale* but also in *The House of Fame*, *The Parliament of Fowls*, *The Franklin's Tale*, the *Troilus* again, and in an unfinished poem called *Anelida and Arcite*. The last appears to be a first attempt at a self-contained translation from the *Teseida*, though in it Chaucer shows more interest in the 'epic' style of Boccaccio's poem than in its story.

The *Teseida* was written in 1339–40. It too had an 'old story' as its source, the *Thebaid* of Statius (which Chaucer also made some use of), but Boccaccio's treatment of it was intended not only to produce a modern version of classical epic poetry, but also to appeal directly to his mistress,

Maria d'Aquino, in order to regain her favour. The part of the story that concerns Palamon and Arcite was probably invented by Boccaccio himself, and Emilia (Chaucer's Emelye) was intended to stand for Maria, while Boccaccio was represented by one of the two knights, though modern scholars do not agree which one. Chaucer's poem did not have any private purpose of this kind, and in general his 'translation' from Boccaccio is very different from the literal rendering that we in the twentieth century understand by the word. He transmutes his source, to an extent which is most obvious in the fact that he reduces its length from nearly 10,000 lines to 2250. He makes in effect a new poem, a reinterpretation of the old story which is thoroughly and unmistakably Chaucerian. Much scholarly commentary on *The Knight's Tale* has been devoted to elucidating its exact relationship to its source, both in detail and in overall purpose. In this edition not much commentary of this kind will be found, because, though interesting in itself, it is not necessarily relevant to a study of Chaucer's own work, and may even distract attention from it. It must be remembered that the original audience of *The Knight's Tale* would almost certainly not have known the *Teseida*, or even perhaps its story, and they would therefore have had to deduce Chaucer's meaning simply from what he himself had written. If Chaucer's intentions had emerged only from a comparison of his poem with its source, he would have failed. I shall therefore refer to the *Teseida* only when comparison seems to clarify specific points, rather than use it as a permanent guiding star.

In *The General Prologue* to *The Canterbury Tales*, the group of pilgrims, including Chaucer himself, who are about to set out from the Tabard Inn in Southwark for the shrine of St Thomas à Becket at Canterbury agree to the suggestion of Harry Bailly, landlord of the Tabard, that they should pass away the time on their journey by telling stories to each other. On the morning when they depart, Harry proposes that they should draw lots to decide who is to tell the first story. They do so, and, 'Were it by aventure, or sort, or cas', the lot falls to the Knight. The chance event is highly appropriate, for the Knight is the person of highest social rank among the pilgrims, and he immediately agrees to begin. The tale he tells is the poem with which we are concerned in this book.

But the poem we call *The Knight's Tale* did not begin life as the first of *The Canterbury Tales*. In another of Chaucer's poems, dating probably from the middle 1380's, the Prologue to *The Legend of Good Women*, Chaucer is defended by Alcestis against the charge of having committed heresy against Cupid. She lists the works he has written in praise of love, and includes among them

> ...al the love of Palamon and Arcite
> Of Thebes, thogh the storye is knowen lite.

This must undoubtedly be an earlier version of *The Knight's Tale*, though of course we do not know how different it may have been from the poem we now have. But this reference to the work, indicating that it once existed separately, may help us to understand what kind of poem *The Knight's Tale* is. *The Legend of Good Women* is essentially a court poem, and may even have been written at the request of the Queen herself. Up to the time when he undertook *The Canterbury Tales*, Chaucer was primarily a court poet, writing in the first place for a small aristocratic audience, though his poems may later have circulated more widely in manuscript. One of the early manuscripts of *Troilus and Criseyde* (which dates from the early 1380's, and is also referred to in the Prologue to the *Legend*) has an illustration showing Chaucer himself, standing in a kind of pulpit, reading his poem aloud to the brilliant and sophisticated court of Richard II. The 'love of Palamon and Arcite' must date from roughly the same period as the *Troilus*, and was probably written for this kind of audience, while *The Canterbury Tales*, in which it was later included, was probably put together with a wider audience in mind.

LEGEND AND MODERNITY

It is clear at least how *The Knight's Tale* would appeal to the narrower circle of a court audience. It is a thoroughly aristocratic poem, dealing with the two main interests and, in theory at least, the two main activities of medieval courtiers—love and war. It would have been, from the point of view of the audience I have postulated, a thoroughly contemporary poem. This may sound an odd thing to say of a work supposedly set in the remote classical past. The story begins at the point of intersection of two great bodies of ancient Greek legend—that concerning the hero Theseus, and that concerning the city of Thebes. After Theseus had killed the Minotaur in Crete, he became king of Athens. He then led an expedition against the Amazons, a tribe of warlike women, defeated them, and returned to Athens with their queen as his bride. (In *The Knight's Tale* the queen is called Ypolita, and Emelye is her younger sister.) Meanwhile the series of events called 'the seven against Thebes' had been taking place. The twin brothers Polyneices and Eteocles had been made joint kings of Thebes, but Eteocles had banished Polyneices. Polyneices then gathered seven champions to support him (including the Capaneus mentioned in *The Knight's Tale*, 74), and they led an expedition against Thebes. After the twins had killed each other, the expedition was defeated by Creon, their uncle, with great loss of life. Creon then became ruler of Thebes, and refused to allow the bodies of his dead enemies to be buried, but left them to be eaten by dogs. This is the legendary background to the story of *The Knight's Tale*, which actually begins with Theseus on his triumphant return to Athens being accosted by a party of the widows of those killed in the attack on Thebes.

Thus the story of Arcite and Palamon, though not itself of classical origin, is carefully related to the legendary classical past, and Theseus, a leading figure in ancient Greek legend, remains one of its central characters. Chaucer occasionally reminds us of the antiquity of this setting. He begins, vaguely enough, with the line already quoted—'Whilom, as olde stories tellen us.' He tells us that the widows carried out funeral rites for their dead husbands 'as was tho the gyse' (135)—that is, by burning them, not by the medieval Christian practice of burial. This ancient custom of cremation is described in more detail at the funeral of Arcite (1995–2054), where there is also a reference to the hamadryads and other local spirits of Greek mythology. But the chief classical gods, though they play a most important part in the action, are absorbed, as we shall see, into the planets of medieval astrology; and in general Chaucer conceives his story in medieval terms. Like medieval painters of historical scenes, who dress the figures in the costume of the painter's time, he finds in the past fame and exoticism but little of antiquarian interest. At one point he justifies himself, in passing, for a medievalization of costume, when, after listing in detail the medieval armour and weapons carried by the knights in the tournament, he adds with significant casualness 'Ther is no newe gyse that it nas old' (1267). As a result of this attitude, Theseus becomes the 'duc' of Athens, Palamon and Arcite become medieval knights, and Emelye becomes a medieval lady, going a-Maying with 'Hir yelow heer... broided in a tresse / Bihinde hir bak, a yerde long' (191–2).

This 'medievalization' of the story (which for Chaucer, if he had considered it consciously, would have been a modernization, a bringing up-to-date) is worth pausing over, because so much of our understanding of the poem depends on our recognition of the ways in which it assumes specifically medieval codes of behaviour. It is particularly noticeable in the Tale's two main subjects, war and love.

MEDIEVAL WAR

To take war first: the martial activities of the poem can frequently be paralleled from medieval chronicles, and must often be interpreted according to medieval conceptions of the laws of war, which are very different from our own. Theseus's campaign against the Thebans follows medieval customs exactly. He begins by 'displaying' his banner, which was a conventional sign that open war had been declared. Then battle takes place in a field outside the city, the defenders are beaten and retreat within its walls, they are pursued, and the victors finally destroy the city utterly. The action sounds barbarous, but the destruction of a besieged city taken by assault was permitted by the law of war, and was frequently carried out. Afterwards the pillagers search the battlefield, and they recognize Palamon and Arcite by their 'cote-armures' (158), the medieval signs of identity among the noble. The two knights are brought to Theseus, and he sends them to prison for life. Chaucer three times mentions a detail not found in his source, that Theseus would accept no ransom for them. Here again an understanding in medieval terms is necessary, for to gain money by ransom was a major and legitimate purpose of medieval warfare. Theseus is therefore acting with extraordinary singlemindedness, and, we may even be intended to understand, with extraordinary nobility. When the two knights meet for their secret duel, Theseus is outraged that they should be fighting 'Withouten juge or oother officere' (854). This too is a medieval reaction, for a fight to the death among noble combatants was considered legal in the Middle Ages only if conducted under the control of heralds. The appeal of the onlooking ladies to Theseus to have mercy, and Theseus's agreement to it, represent not merely a fantasy of ideal nobility but a possible medieval reality. In a famous case, Edward III's queen had interceded with the king to have mercy on six citizens of Calais whose lives were legitimately forfeit, and her appeal had been successful. The tournament by which the claim to Emelye's hand is to be settled, though no doubt made more magnificent by poetic licence, also reflects a genuine late-medieval love of spectacle, and follows the pattern of actual tournaments as recorded by the chroniclers. The regulations as modified by Theseus to limit weapons to the spear and sword, and to order capture rather than a fight to the death, were those normal in medieval tournaments, and the feasts held before and

7

after were also common accompaniments to tournaments in Chaucer's own time. All this must be understood if we are to recognize the nature of the Tale's appeal to its original audience and to interpret it correctly.

The medieval nature of Chaucer's treatment of love is even more crucial to an understanding of *The Knight's Tale*, and is perhaps more likely to be misunderstood by modern readers. I have remarked that love was one of the main interests and activities of medieval courtly society; but it was specifically 'courtly love', love of a very distinct kind.[1] The theory at least of courtly love turned love into a code, a game to be played elegantly according to definite rules. The art of love was set down somewhat cynically for aristocratic readers in the enormously influential French poem, the *Roman de la Rose*, which Chaucer had translated into English at an early stage of his poetic career. In this, the course of a love affair is described allegorically in the form of a dream, in which the Dreamer first finds his way into a rose-garden. This is the garden of love, and it is noticeable that certain unpleasant aspects of human life are explicitly excluded from it—poverty and old age for example. In *The Knight's Tale*, similarly, the setting is exclusively aristocratic and untroubled by problems of money or time. Arcite, disguised as Philostrate, is given by Theseus 'gold to maintene his degree', and also goes on secretly receiving his 'rente' from 'his contree' (583–5),

[1] Since this section was first written, scholars have cast doubt on the validity of the term 'courtly love' and of the whole underlying conception. The argument is not yet at an end, but for some recent views see *The Meaning of Courtly Love*, ed. F. X. Newman (State University of New York Press, 1968) and E. T. Donaldson, *Speaking of Chaucer* (Athlone Press, 1970), chapter 11.

while despite the passage of many years in the course of
the story, there is no indication that Palamon and Emelye
have become any less attractive or desirable at the end of it.
Inside the garden, the Dreamer finds the God of Love
himself, leading Beauty by the hand and accompanied by
a whole train of allegorical figures, including Idleness, the
gatekeeper of the garden. At the centre of the garden is
a spring forming a pool by which Narcissus died for love
of his own reflexion. In *The Knight's Tale* Idleness, now
gatekeeper to the garden of Venus, the goddess of love, is
mentioned in the description of the Temple of Venus, and
Narcissus also appears in the same description (1082–3).
As the Dreamer in the *Roman de la Rose* bends to admire
a rose-bud in the garden, the God of Love shoots an
arrow at him which wounds his heart through his eye.
The head of the arrow, which will not come out of the
wound, is called Beauty, and the rose-bud is the girl with
whom he falls in love. Exactly the same pattern of ideas
recurs in *The Knight's Tale* when Palamon first sees
Emelye wandering in the garden from his prison window.
He falls in love with her at first sight, and the effect is of a
sudden sickness or wound.

> He cast his eye upon Emelya,
> And therwithal he bleynte and cride, 'A!'
> As though he stongen were unto the herte. (219-21)

Arcite then looks at Emelye too,

> Wher as this lady romed to and fro,
> And with that sighte hir beautee hurte him so,
> That, if that Palamon was wounded sore,
> Arcite is hurt as muche as he, or moore.
> And with a sigh he seyde pitously:
> 'The fresshe beautee sleeth me sodeynly
> Of hire that rometh in the yonder place.' (255–61)

Emelye's beauty is killing him; and the same idea recurs with greater intensity when, disguised as Philostrate, he has returned to Athens, and soliloquizes while Palamon secretly listens:

> And over al this, to sleen me outrely,
> Love hath his firy dart so brenningly
> Ystiked thurgh my trewe, careful herte,
> That shapen was my deeth erst than my sherte.
> Ye sleen me with youre eyen, Emelye;
> Ye been the cause wherfore that I die.   (705–10)

The wound given by Love's arrow is mortal. For courtiers playing the game of love this was no doubt only a metaphor, but for Arcite it is literally true: he is killed by his love for Emelye, after the tournament at the end of the poem.

The conception of love as an injury received through the eye, incurable and perhaps mortal, is basic to the whole story of *The Knight's Tale*. Arcite and Palamon have no choice but to behave as they do; they *must* love Emelye, whatever extravagance or absurdity their love may lead them into, because they are suffering from a sickness. The love-poetry of the Middle Ages and the Renaissance is full of disease imagery: an attack of love is like a bout of influenza and has many of the same symptoms. Love as a disease also appears in *The Knight's Tale*. When Arcite is banished from Athens and hence from Emelye, he cannot eat, drink, or sleep, and he becomes so pale and thin as to be unrecognizable. Chaucer treats love as a disease with the greatest seriousness and literalness, explaining in physiological terms how 'the loveris maladye / Of Hereos' (i.e. Eros) leads to mania (515–16). Another symptom of love according to courtly theory is moodiness, and this too is displayed by Arcite when, after singing a gay song, he falls suddenly 'into a studie' (672), which results in his soliloquy just referred to. The genesis and development of the two lovers' feelings would be followed by a courtly audience in a spirit of connoisseurship, as they watched the enactment in fictional reality of the game they played themselves somewhere between jest and seriousness. Since the code of love was so exactly defined, a casuistry of love had been developed, and there could be lengthy argument on such questions as whether one lover's situation was more or less happy than another's. Just such a problem or *demande d'amour* is put directly to his audience by the Knight at the end of Part I of the Tale:

> Yow loveres axe I now this questioun:
> Who hath the worse, Arcite or Palamoun?
> That oon may seen his lady day by day,
> But in prison he moot dwelle alway;
> That oother wher him list may ride or go,
> But seen his lady shal he nevere mo.
> Now demeth as yow liste, ye that kan,
> For I wol telle forth as I bigan.   (489–96)

The audience addressed here is surely one of courtiers rather than pilgrims, for courtiers were lovers by profession, and in *Troilus and Criseyde* a courtly audience is addressed in exactly the same way as experts on love.

The lady and the season

So much for the symptoms of love in the lover. What of the lady he loves? Medieval courtly love is often a one-way affair: it is seen from the point of view of the man, whose feelings are of great interest and may be analysed at length, while the woman exists only as an object arousing

those feelings. The arrow is shot in one direction only.
So it is in *The Knight's Tale*. The feelings of Emelye are
never considered at all. In the *Roman de la Rose* we see
everything through the eyes of the Dreamer who falls in
love, and the girl he loves is a rose-bud, part of the Maytime setting of the poem. Palamon and Arcite also fall in
love in May, while Emelye is gathering flowers in a
garden. And Emelye appears less as a person than as a
personification of the Maytime garden: this is the effect of
the imagery by which she is first described—

> Till it fil ones, in a morwe of May,
> That Emelye, that fairer was to sene
> Than is the lilie upon his stalke grene,
> And fressher than the May with floures newe—
> For with the rose colour stroof hire hewe,
> I noot which was the finer of hem two. (176–81)

She is not quite an allegorical rose, but she looks very like
one: an almost purely symbolic figure. A garden in May
becomes the regular setting for love in medieval courtly
poetry, and the events of *The Knight's Tale* seem to take
place in a perpetual May. It is May when Palamon and
Arcite fall in love, and Emelye has gone out 'to doon
honour to Maye' (189)—to take part in the courtly seasonal
ritual of going out early to sing and gather flowers and
leaves, a ceremony in which the poem's audience would
also regularly participate. It is May again, seven years
later, when Arcite, as Philostrate, has gone out

> To maken him a gerland of the greves
> Were it of wodebinde or hawethorn leves,
> And loude he song ayeyn the sonne shene:
> 'May, with alle thy floures and thy grene,
> Welcome be thou, faire, fresshe May,
> In hope that I som grene gete may' (649–54)

and is overheard by Palamon. It is because Theseus loves hunting in May that he discovers the two fighting next day. And it is exactly one year later, and therefore still in May, that the lovers are brought together again and the lark is singing just as it did the year before.[1] As Palamon rises to pray to Venus,

> Up roos the sonne, and up roos Emelye.　　(1415)

She remains little more than a personification of the feelings associated with spring, the crystallization of an atmosphere. Later in the same day, the fatal tournament takes place, and we are told that

> Greet was the feeste in Atthenes that day,
> And eek the lusty seson of that May
> Made every wight to been in swich pleasaunce
> That al that Monday justen they and daunce,
> And spenden it in Venus heigh servise.　　(1625–9)

But by now the joy of May has come to seem deceptive.

The religion of love

Though Emelye is thus a figure of no interest whatsoever as a person, she is given great power by the love her beauty arouses. Love, after all, is a god in the *Roman de la Rose*, and the code of love developed in courtly society into a religion of love. This religion was a parody of Christianity, borrowing its conceptions and terminology, and it is constantly played against Christianity in Chaucer's poetry. If taken seriously the religion of courtly love would have been a heretical rival to the true religion, and indeed it has been suggested that its historical origin is connected with the development of heretical cults in

---

[1] Compare ll. 633–4 with 1351–4.

southern France in the twelfth century. But in fourteenth-
century England this religion too was a game, an unsyste-
matic collection of attitudes. Sometimes the object of the
cult was the lady herself, and so when Palamon first sees
Emelye he does not know whether she is human or divine.
This is the traditional response of the lover to the first
sight of the beloved, though Palamon, being conceived of
at this point as a pagan, thinks she may be the goddess
Venus. If the lady is thought of as her lover's goddess,
then he can deserve no benefit at her hands, as if she were
his equal. On this point a theology of courtly love is
developed, paralleling Christian theology. Just as man
can be saved not by justice (for all men deserve damnation
for the sin of Adam) but only by God's mercy or grace, so
the courtly lover must beg for a response to his love from
his lady's mercy. Thus Arcite says, on first seeing Emelye:

> And but I have hir mercy and hir grace,
> That I may seen hire atte leeste weye,
> I nam but deed; ther nis namoore to seye. (262–4)

And, at the very end of the poem, when Theseus is per-
suading Emelye to marry Palamon, he argues that Palamon has long served her and suffered for her, and 'gentil
mercy oghte to passen right' (2231). Arcite has claimed
no greater mercy of Emelye than to see her. Now in
Christian theology the sight of God *is* heaven, or at least
the chief reward of the blessed, and the deprivation of this
sight is the chief punishment of the damned. This too has
its parallel in the religion of love, and so later when Arcite
has been freed from prison but banished from Athens, and
hence from Emelye's presence, he argues that now he is
in hell eternally, while in prison he would have been in
heavenly bliss. As a result of this deprivation of the sight

of his lady, he can expect to die in *wanhope*—despair, the ultimate sin in Christian terms, which makes salvation impossible.

The parody-theology mentioned so far has made the lady the god of the religion of love. But there is a different parody-theology which places the God of Love himself in this position, and this too comes into *The Knight's Tale*. The medieval God of Love is Cupid; it is sometimes remembered that in classical mythology Cupid is the son of Venus, but the medieval Cupid is usually very different from the pretty boy of Roman statuary or modern Valentines. He is a lord, a tyrant even (so he is accused of being in the Prologue to *The Legend of Good Women*), and terrifying in the power he possesses over his devotees. This view of Cupid is developed most fully in Theseus' long speech when he finds Palamon and Arcite fighting in the woods, the speech beginning

> The god of love, a, *benedicite!*
> How mighty and how greet a lord is he!
> Ayeyns his might ther gaineth none obstacles.
> He may be cleped a god for his miracles....
> Bihoold, for Goddes sake that sit above,
> Se how they blede! (927–30, 942–3)

The apparently incongruous 'for Goddes sake that sit above'—a reference to the Christian God—is not an accidental anachronism, for Theseus goes on to emphasize that the service of Cupid really is folly, a folly exemplified in the way these two are striving to murder each other for the sake of a woman who doesn't even know of their existence. The contrast between the religion of Cupid and the true religion is a common one, made more piquant by the fact that Christianity is a religion of love and that the Christian God could also be called a God of Love. The

contrast is wittily expressed in an earlier line, an exclamation by the narrator when Palamon and Arcite agree to
fight: 'O Cupide, out of alle charitee!' (765). The line
means simply 'O Cupid, lacking in all kindness', but it includes a play on the two kinds of love, *charitee* (Latin *caritas*)
or Christian love, and *cupiditas*, the evil self-love of mere
desire.

Love and friendship

But the relationship, fraught with paradoxes, between the
two religions and the two loves is not much explored in
The Knight's Tale: it is a more central theme of other
courtly poems by Chaucer, and particularly of *Troilus and
Criseyde*. A contrast which is more persistent, and more
significant, in *The Knight's Tale* is that between love and
friendship, *amor* and *amicitia*. Just as love was formalized
and codified in medieval courtly society, so might friendship be; and the carefully defined friendship between
Palamon and Arcite is a more important theme in the poem
than the modern reader may perhaps realize. The two
are cousins by birth, but they are also 'sworn brothers'—
that is, they have sworn to treat each other as brothers, as
Palamon explains:

> That nevere, for to dyen in the peyne,
> Til that the deeth departe shal us tweyne,
> Neither of us in love to hindre oother,
> Ne in noon oother cas, my leeve brother;
> But that thou sholdest trewely forthren me
> In every cas, as I shal forthren thee.   (275–80)

But when they are both struck by the irresistible force
of love for Emelye, there necessarily develops a conflict
between their love and their brotherhood. Palamon claims
that Arcite's oath of brotherhood binds him to assist him in

his pursuit of Emelye, but Arcite answers by asserting a theory that love is above all laws, precisely because it cannot be resisted:

> I pose that thow lovedest hire biforn;
> Wostow nat wel the olde clerkes sawe,
> That 'who shal yeve a lovere any lawe?'
> Love is a gretter lawe, by my pan,
> Than may be yeve to any erthely man;
> And therfore positif lawe and swich decree
> Is broken al day for love in ech degree.
> A man moot nedes love, maugree his heed.
> He may nat fleen it thogh he sholde be deed.
>
> (304–12)

They go through the same arguments at a later stage of the poem. When Palamon overhears Arcite soliloquizing on his love for Emelye, he breaks in angrily with

> Arcite, false traitour wikke,
> Now artow hent, that lovest my lady so,
> For whom that I have al this peyne and wo,
> And art my blood, and to my conseil sworn,
> As I ful ofte have told thee heerbiforn.   (722–6)

And Arcite's answer is:

> For I defye the seurete and the bond
> Which that thou seist that I have maad to thee.
> What, verray fool, think wel that love is free,
> And I wol love hire maugree al thy might!   (746–9)

Amicitia remains powerful, however, and prevents Arcite from killing Palamon on the spot; instead they arrange a formal combat for the next day, and before it

> Everich of hem heelp for to armen oother
> As freendly as he were his owene brother.   (793–4)

And at the very end of the poem, there is a sense in which *amicitia* triumphs, for Arcite in his dying speech does not, as we might expect, curse Palamon, but recommends him to Emelye if she should ever marry. Friendship could scarcely go further, and we feel (and are perhaps meant to feel) that it is more noble than love. *Amor* is an all-powerful force operating on men from outside, but *amicitia* is a willed human response by which man may achieve a spiritual triumph in the very moment of bodily defeat.

Marriage

There remains one last point to be made concerning the treatment of love in *The Knight's Tale*. I remarked that courtly love began in a feudal society where marriage was regarded as a property transaction and had no connexion with love. Marriage is not regarded in this way in *The Knight's Tale*, where, as in other poems by Chaucer, it is seen as the natural consummation of a courtly love affair. But marriage remains on a different footing from love, in the sense that whereas love is a private and even secret affair, the marriage of noble persons is a public matter. Theseus proposes the marriage of Emelye to Palamon as the result of

> ...a parlement
> At Atthenes upon certein pointz and caas;
> Among the whiche pointz yspoken was
> To have with certein contrees alliaunce,
> And have fully of Thebans obeisaunce. (2112-16)

And when he finally makes the proposal, at the end of his long philosophical speech, he is careful to say that he does so 'with al th'avis heere of my parlement' (2218). This is certainly true to the realities of life among the aristocracy in fourteenth-century England.

'GENTILLESSE'

Besides the specific matters of love and war, *The Knight's Tale* reflects the attitudes of medieval courtly society to human behaviour in general. The poem's highest ethical quality is *gentillesse*, a word which may be roughly translated as 'nobility', but which has no exact equivalent in modern English, because it depends for its meaning on a social background which has completely changed. *Gentillesse* is at once a social and an ethical quality. It is the kind of behaviour—magnanimous, generous, and unselfish—that would be expected of people of high birth, and that high birth would ideally produce. Medieval people knew as well as we do, of course, that aristocratic birth and breeding do not automatically produce noble behaviour; but they felt that they ought to. All the main characters of *The Knight's Tale*, without exception, are of the highest aristocracy, related to the royal houses of Thebes or Athens. Even the widows who accost Theseus at the beginning of the poem are duchesses or queens, and their descent to misery is felt to be the more moving because of this. It is of course his *gentillesse* that they appeal to. When Arcite is disguised as Philostrate, and is serving as page of Emelye's chamber, even in this comparatively humble situation,

> He was so gentil of condicioun
> That thurghout al the court was his renoun.
>
> (573–4)

And, with his dying breath, Arcite recommends Palamon to Emelye as *gentil*: 'Foryet nat Palamon, the gentil man (1939)'. *Gentillesse* obviously embraces a number of different virtues—it is more a general disposition than a distinct

quality—and some of these are listed just before this in
Arcite's dying speech, when he enumerates Palamon's
virtues as a lover. But a central virtue in *gentillesse* is *pitee*,
pity or compassion, and this plays a key role in the poem.
One of the great innovations of medieval Christianity, with
its concentration on the human sufferings of Christ, was to
make compassion one of the most highly valued virtues.
To feel Christ's sufferings as if they were one's own, to
share the sympathetic agony of Mary and John at the foot
of the cross—these are the great goals set up by medieval
devotional writings. And as the Middle Ages progressed,
this concentration on suffering and pity for suffering became more and more intensified, and, to modern tastes,
excessive. It extended into secular writings, naturally, and
late medieval literature and art generally show definite
tendencies towards sentimentality—a flow of emotion
produced too easily and indulged in for its own sake.
Chaucer was a man of his age in the high value he gave to
pitee, and some of his favourite scenes seem to have been
those of pathos, in which spectators within the poem
dissolve into compassionate tears, which the reader or
listener is clearly intended to share. The final scenes of
The Clerk's Tale (when Grisilde's supposedly dead children are restored to her) and of *The Prioress's Tale* (when
the little boy dies) may be mentioned as examples. But
Chaucer was well aware of the dangers of *pitee* dispropor-
tionate to its object, as is shown by the satirical description
of the Prioress in *The General Prologue*, who

> ...was so charitable and so *pitous*
> She wolde wepe, if that she saugh a mous
> Kaught in a trappe, if it were deed or bledde.

> (142-4)

In *The Knight's Tale, pitee* plays a central part without ever running to excess. When the widows appeal to Theseus's *gentillesse*, it is in *pitee* that they expect it to be displayed:

> Som drope of pitee, thurgh thy gentillesse,
> Upon us wrecched wommen lat thou falle.   (62–3)

At the end of their appeal,

> This gentil duc doun from his courser sterte
> With herte pitous, whan he herde hem speke.
> Him thoughte that his herte wolde breke.   (94–6)

Theseus seems to be the poem's chief embodiment of *pitee*, and there is a similar scene later when he discovers Palamon and Arcite fighting and impulsively sentences them both to death. This time it is the queen and her ladies who fall on their knees and appeal to him, for 'Greet pitee was it, as it thoughte hem alle' (893). Again he succumbs to a feminine appeal for mercy, and his softening is justified by the Knight with a general statement that again associates *pitee* with *gentillesse*: 'For pitee renneth soone in gentil herte' (903). The sentiment was clearly near to Chaucer's heart, for he uses exactly the same line, word for word, at three other places in his works: and it was indeed a common sentiment among medieval writers generally.

PAGEANTRY

A last respect in which *The Knight's Tale* reflects medieval, and more specifically late-medieval, courtly attitudes, is its ceremonial or pageant-like quality. The medieval aristocracy had always had a taste for formality and display, expressing itself in elaborate feasts, processions, or tournaments, and in the later Middle Ages this taste became a passion. Spiritual values were expressed in outward grandeur, and aristocratic magnanimity in material extravagance. The aristocratic literary genre to which *The Knight's Tale* belongs, the chivalric romance, naturally reflected this taste through descriptions of feasts and other ceremonial events, and this reflexion appears in an extreme form in *The Knight's Tale*. Almost every event in the poem is ceremonial. Many of its events are ceremonies in themselves—Theseus's triumphant march home from his victory over the Amazons, and his march into battle against the Thebans, the Maytime *observaunces* carried out by Emelye in Part I and by Arcite in Part II, and the prayers in the temples of the three gods. There are many ceremonies connected with the tournament: Theseus's feast before it, the processional appearance of the two chief champions, Lygurge and Emetreus (following each other with such symmetry that each is described in exactly twenty-seven lines), and the tournament itself, with the exact equality of the two sides, its careful conduct by the heralds and its definite rules of procedure. Finally there are the funeral of Arcite, and the wedding of Palamon and Emelye. And even events which are not intrinsically ceremonial are turned into ceremonies. The company of widows who appeal to Theseus on his return home might seem a disorderly interruption to his triumph, but in fact they arrange themselves with perfect symmetry—'tweye and tweye, / Ech after oother' (40–1) and only turn the triumph into a ceremony of a different kind, a ritual of pleading and assent. Again, when, amidst the confusion of the battlefield, the bodies of Palamon and Arcite are discovered by the pillagers, they too are arranged symmetrically, 'ligginge by and by, / Bothe in oon armes' (153–4).

More centrally, the quarrel between rival lovers which is the main subject of the poem begins in private and is made more ceremonial by stages. It begins when Palamon overhears Arcite's soliloquy and draws his sword as if to kill him. But an impromptu scuffle will not do, for Palamon is unarmed, and so they arrange to meet more formally next day for a duel in full armour. This meeting is interrupted by Theseus, and he substitutes for the secret duel a full-scale public tournament, with a hundred supporters on each side, to be fought out with the greatest possible formality and magnificence. In *The Knight's Tale* the ceremonial tendencies of chivalric romance are taken about as far as they will go. The poem already moves cumbrously under the weight of its ceremonial encrustation; a little more pageantry and one fears it would cease to move at all.

CONVENTION OF EXTREME EMOTION

The Knight's Tale offers, then, to its original aristocratic audience, an image of the noble life: an image of human life as a noble pageant. It was not perhaps in every respect the life that audience really lived (though we have seen how 'realistically' it mirrors late medieval practices in war, for example), but it was the life they aspired to live. In arriving at this statement, we have already left behind the mere content of the Tale, and begun to describe the way in which that content is treated. Indeed the two aspects of the Tale cannot be sharply distinguished: content and treatment, material and technique, flow into each other, for the selection of material is itself one of the fundamental techniques of literary creation. Having passed this fluid

border, we can now proceed to consider matters which
more obviously belong to the literary technique of the
poem. We have seen that the main characters of *The
Knight's Tale* are all high aristocrats; but how are these
characters presented to us? Chaucer is often described,
perhaps without much thought, as the first English
novelist, but if we look at *The Knight's Tale* we shall find
characters presented in a way utterly different from that
of the novel. For one thing their feelings are presented to
us not with the novelist's fine discrimination, separating
one shade of feeling from another, but through a consis-
tent and non-realistic convention. By this convention, all
feelings are extreme, and are expressed by extreme outward signs. This is most noticeable in the case we have
already touched on, of suffering and the pity it arouses.
This can already be observed in the first incident of the
poem, when Theseus is accosted by the widows. Their
grief is externalized in lamentation, rather than realized
internally as experience, and the lamentation is of an
extreme kind:

> ...swich a cry and swich a wo they make
> That in this world nis creature livinge
> That herde swich another waymentinge.   (42-4)

Crying aloud is one sign of extreme grief; another is losing
consciousness completely, and this too appears in the same
scene, when Theseus asks the reason for their lamentation:

> The eldeste lady of hem alle spak,
> Whan she hadde swowned with a deedly cheere,
> That it was routhe for to seen and heere.   (54-6)

Swoons tend to be presented in this matter-of-course way
as interruptions of the poem's narrative line. The same
thing happens in a later scene, when Arcite, disguised as

24

Philostrate, is soliloquizing about his ignominious situation. He expresses his grief at great length,

> And with that word he fil doun in a traunce
> A longe time, and after he up sterte.   (714–15)

An editor of sixty years ago wrote concerning these lines that Chaucer 'ought not to have seemed to stop the action in order to allow Arcite to faint'. The criticism seems reasonable, and indeed it would have a great deal of point if we were to consider these and similar lines as realistic accounts of human behaviour. It is true, certainly, that medieval people did allow themselves to express emotion in violent outward signs such as lamenting and perhaps even fainting more readily than people (at least in northern Europe) do nowadays. But, even when this is allowed for, it must be recognized that this way of presenting emotion belongs to an essentially non-realistic literary convention. By this convention, *all* emotions are heightened, so that the swoon becomes a kind of shorthand for expressing intense grief (as here) or, equally, intense joy (as when Grisilde in *The Clerk's Tale* is reunited to her children). A medieval reader, familiar with the convention, would never have considered how much time the swoon took up.

A further sign of intense grief is internal rather than external, in the sense that it takes the form of an intention rather than a deed, but it is none the less conventional. This is the threat to commit suicide. When Arcite is released from prison but banished from Athens, his reaction is described as follows:

> How greet a sorwe suffreth now Arcite!
> The deeth he feeleth thurgh his herte smite;
> He wepeth, waileth, crieth pitously;
> To sleen himself he waiteth prively.   (361–4)

The first of these lines asserts the extreme quality of his feelings. The second emphasizes this extreme quality by relating it to death through the conventional image of a sword cutting (compare the arrow of love, which also deals a mortal wound). The third externalizes the emotion in the three outward forms of weeping, wailing and crying—an utterly perfunctory indication of grief which can be paralleled many times over in Chaucer's works. The fourth adds the intention to commit suicide in secret. But there is no indication, here or elsewhere, of any practical effect of this search for an opportunity to kill himself. Considered as a piece of realism, it is not in the least credible; but it is clearly not intended as a piece of realism. There is an even more striking example of the same convention in *The Franklin's Tale*, when the heroine, having got herself into a situation where she cannot avoid being unfaithful to her husband, says several times that she would prefer death, gives a list of examples of women who have died rather than submit to dishonour, laments for 'a day or tweye, / Purposinge evere that she wolde deye', but still does not in fact commit suicide, or show any sign of attempting to do so. Clearly in such cases we have to deal not with a lifelike account of actual human behaviour but with a convention which presents emotion symbolically in a heightened form. This convention includes joy as well as sorrow, though joy is less common in *The Knight's Tale*. But when Theseus ordains that Palamon and Arcite shall fight in a tournament for Emelye in a year's time, the general reaction is one of joy, and it is described as follows:

> Who looketh lightly now but Palamoun?
> Who springeth up for joye but Arcite?
> Who kouthe telle, or who kouthe it endite,

26

The joye that is maked in the place
Whan Theseus hath doon so fair a grace?
But doun on knees wente every maner wight,
And thonked him with al hir herte and might,
And namely the Thebans often sithe.   (1012–19)

Again the emotion is extreme, and again it is externalized, in cheerful looks, jumping up, kneeling, and multiple expressions of thanks.

THE CHARACTERS

Theseus

If this is how all the characters of the Tale are presented as feeling and expressing their emotions, then there is unlikely to be any subtle distinction between the characters on the level of their internal experience. Thus another of the novel's sources of interest is excluded. There are four main characters in *The Knight's Tale*: Theseus, Emelye, Palamon, and Arcite. Of these the most distinct as a personality is perhaps Theseus: he is lordly, courageous, impulsive (witness his immediate response to the widows' appeal and his immediate death sentence on the two lovers when he finds them fighting), yet open to the appeal of friendship (Perotheus), womanly pity, or reason (his cancellation of the death sentence on the lovers). He is older and more mature than the other characters, reflective, and wise. Yet even when we have said all this, we are still very little aware of Theseus as a distinct personality. We have only to compare him with a character from a nineteenth- or twentieth-century historical novel, or even with one of Shakespeare's rulers—Duncan or Claudius—to recognize that our interest is not in him as an individual. It is rather, we may say provisionally, in him as part of a literary structure embodying a certain significance, a certain view of life.

Palamon and Arcite

The story focuses its main attention upon Palamon and Arcite, and in general the way in which they are presented is in line with the symmetry with which they are introduced. If one were to approach the Tale with the same expectations as in reading a novel, one might expect to find a carefully worked out and subtly depicted difference of character between the two knights. In this case, one would be disappointed. As characters, they are scarcely distinguishable. We first hear them speak in Theseus's prison. Palamon sees Emelye from the window, and immediately falls in love with her. Then Arcite sees her,

> And with that sighte hir beautee hurte him so,
> That, if that Palamon was wounded sore,
> Arcite is hurt as muche as he, or moore.   (256–8)

The whole point, clearly, is that their reactions are exactly the same. As a result, they quarrel, Palamon saying that he 'loved' her first, and accusing Arcite of breaking his oath of brotherhood by failing to aid him in this love. Arcite offers two lines of defence against this accusation. The first is that, though Palamon saw Emelye first, *he* loved her first 'paramour' (by way of human love). He points out that Palamon's first reaction was to wonder whether Emelye was a woman or a goddess, and so, he says,

> Thyn is affeccioun of hoolinesse,
> And myn is love, as to a creature.   (300–1)

Some modern scholars have seen a profound significance in this distinction between human and divine love; it has

been argued that it reflects a difference of character between the two knights, one being a practical schemer, the
other an idealistic dreamer. It has even been claimed that
they represent allegorically the active and contemplative
lives of medieval devotional writings. But in context it
seems clear that Arcite's assertion is no more than an
ingenious debating point, for he immediately abandons it
and goes on to his second line of defence, saying, 'Suppose
you did love her first; don't you know that love is a
necessity above all laws?' This seems to be a more
serious argument—Arcite develops it at greater length
than the first—and also one whose truth is displayed in
the working out of the story. For first we see love breaking
the 'law' established between the two knights by their
oath of brotherhood, and then we see it causing both of
them to break a 'law' established between them and
Theseus. Arcite, having been released, illicitly returns to
Athens, and Palamon illicitly breaks out of prison. They
then break a further law by engaging in a duel privately,
without officers or witnesses, and it is only Theseus's
generosity in allowing the dispute between them to be
settled in a formal tournament that brings their quarrel
within the bounds of law again. In all this it is clear that
the focus of our interest is not in the characters as individuals, but in a general idea about human life: that love
is an irresistible force and by being irresistible sets itself
against all laws, and can only with great difficulty be
brought within lawful ceremony.

There is no doubt intended to be a connexion between
Palamon's initial feeling that Emelye may be the goddess
Venus and the fact that before the tournament he prays
to Venus for Emelye, while Arcite prays to Mars for

victory. Venus and Mars are the gods of the two main aristocratic interests of love and war, and Palamon inclines towards one of these while Arcite inclines towards the other. Thus when Emelye prays to Diana that, if she must be given to one of the two knights, she should be given to the one who most desires her, her prayer is granted, and she is given to Palamon, who had set Venus above Mars. Similarly, Arcite gains the victory he desires, while Palamon gains the lady he desires, and so their prayers too are granted, though not as they expected. But none of this elaborate patterning throws much light on the characters of the two knights. We cannot see them even as human individuals embodying opposed moral abstractions, as Elinor Dashwood embodies sense and Marianne Dashwood sensibility in Jane Austen's novel. In the novel, it is through entering sympathetically and critically into the characters' minds that we come to understand what 'sense' and 'sensibility' are; and the characters themselves change bit by bit, so that we see Elinor acquiring more sensibility and Marianne much more sense. In *The Knight's Tale* there are no such processes of sympathetic understanding or moral change. Venus and Mars are forces so powerful as to reduce those through whom they operate to indistinguishability. It cannot be said, I think, that we care which of the knights, as a person, eventually wins Emelye.

Emelye

This is all the more true because Emelye herself, the last of the four central characters, is even less an individual than the other three. We know nothing whatsoever of her character, except that, like all noble ladies, she feels *pitee* easily, and that, like all virgins according to the convention in which the poem is written, she would prefer not to get married. I have said that she appears less as a person than as a personification of the May-morning convention. As such, she is a powerful figure, but once she has served to arouse love in the two knights, she recedes into the background, and she eventually obeys Theseus's advice to marry Palamon without saying a word. Indeed, her only words in the whole poem are her prayer to Diana.

From all this, it should be clear that the meaning of *The Knight's Tale* is not conveyed through characterization. It is something more general, more like a perception of the nature of the human condition as a whole; what that perception is we shall return to consider later. But for the moment it must be said that the lack of interest which the poem demands for its characters as individuals, together with the general nature of its meaning, does not imply that it is a poem without human feeling. Feelings may be aroused for typical human situations as much as for individuals, and there are many moments in the poem—the widows' statement of their plight, the brotherly arming of Palamon and Arcite before their duel, the solitariness and generosity of Arcite in his death—which move us deeply. At such moments we become aware not of the suffering of individuals in whom we are interested for the sake of their individuality, but of the pathos of the general human situation, a situation in which we ourselves are involved by our birth.

INTERRUPTIONS OF THE NARRATIVE

Perhaps then our interest is to be aroused by the narrative itself, as in thrillers with perfunctory characterization where we are mainly excited by the wish to know what will happen next. We shall not have to read very far into the poem to recognize that this cannot be so. The poem has indeed a clear narrative line, not of a haphazard kind but following a definite and simple pattern. The story itself could be told in a few paragraphs, or a few lines. It has been expanded to over 2000 lines, to become the second longest of *The Canterbury Tales*, shorter only than the Parson's concluding prose sermon. As a result the pace of the narrative is enormously slow, and it is constantly interrupted by passages that cannot be considered essential from the point of view of the action. At every opportunity, the characters make long and elaborate speeches, which take them far beyond exposition of their present feelings and intentions into considerations of a more general kind. We may mention as examples Arcite's lament for his situation in Part I, which turns into a philosophical account of the human condition (365–416); the speech of Palamon immediately following this, in which he too turns philosopher and arraigns divine providence (423–75); Theseus's discourse on love in Part II (927–67); Saturn's statement of his powers (1595–1611); and Theseus's philosophical speech at the end of the whole poem, in which he returns to the questions raised by Arcite and Palamon in Part I (2129–231). Even more noticeably, the action is interrupted again and again by elaborate descriptions: for example, of Emelye and the garden in which she is seen by the two knights (176–97);

of Arcite's sickness (500–21); of the tournament (1741–77) and then of Arcite's agony (1885–903) and funeral (1995–2106). The main concentration of descriptive passages comes in Part III, which indeed consists almost entirely of description—of the lists and the three temples erected by Theseus, with all their allegorical decoration, and of Lygurge and Emetreus, the two champions in the tournament. This predominance of description over action is of course connected with the ceremonial quality we have already noted in the poem; it is precisely through description that the effect of ceremony is given. It is also an essential part of the technique of poetry as this was conceived in the Middle Ages. *The Knight's Tale* is in fact as medieval in its technique as in its content. It is constructed according to medieval assumptions about the nature of poems, and in order to understand it more thoroughly, it will be helpful to know something of what these assumptions were.

THE ART OF POETRY

There exist numerous medieval works on the art of poetry, called *artes poeticae*.[1] They are generally school textbooks of an elementary kind, and Chaucer in *The Nun's Priest's Tale* refers to the author of one of them, Geoffroi de Vinsauf, as though it would be a familiar name to his audience. These *artes poeticae* do not contain any very subtle or sophisticated thought on the nature of literature, but they are of great interest for the basic assumptions they state, or sometimes unconsciously imply, about what

[1] For more detailed consideration of the *artes poeticae*, see *An Introduction to Chaucer*, by the editors of this series, ch. 4.

poems are. One of their basic assumptions was implied at the beginning of this Introduction: that the author will be working with a narrative which already exists in some authoritative form and is not to be altered except in detail. We have seen that in *The Knight's Tale* Chaucer begins with the story told by Boccaccio in the *Teseida*, as Boccaccio began with the story told by Statius in the *Thebaid*. Chaucer may alter certain incidents in it, as by making Arcite instead of Palamon see Emelye first, and may subject it to a 'modernizing' process which involves the alteration of certain details, as by making Theseus take Thebes by siege instead of entering it unopposed; but the main outline is given and is unchangeable. It is noticeable that when Chaucer is inventing something of his own he will often pretend that he has it on authority, as he does when he attributes to *olde bookes* the date of 3 May which he himself supplied for Palamon's escape from prison.

The poet is confronted, then, with a particular story, in a particular version, which he has to re-present in his own way. His rehandling of it may involve either abbreviation or amplification; probably both processes will be used in different parts of the material. This is the case in *The Knight's Tale*: the poem as a whole is much shorter than the *Teseida*, but certain parts of it, particularly the philosophical speeches and the descriptions of the temples in Part III, are amplifications of Boccaccio's treatment. The *artes poeticae* list and exemplify various devices by which abbreviation and amplification may be carried out. One abbreviating device, which is much used in *The Knight's Tale*, is what is called *occupatio*—mentioning something only to say that one is not going to describe it further. Thus at the very beginning of the *Tale*, the Knight com-

presses more than a whole book of the *Teseida* into a few
lines by simply mentioning its main events and saying
that he has not time to tell us about them:

> And certes, if it nere to long to heere,
> I wolde have toold yow fully the manere
> How wonnen was the regne of Femenye
> By Theseus and by his chivalrye;
> And of the grete bataille for the nones
> Bitwixen Atthenes and Amazones;
> And how asseged was Ypolita,
> The faire, hardy queene of Scithia;
> And of the feste that was at hir weddinge,
> And of the tempest at hir hoom-cominge;
> But al that thing I moot as now forbere.   (17–27)

Here the *occupatio* is genuine and functional; but it may
also be used in a more sophisticated way to describe even
while seeming to pass over. It is used in this way in the
description of the feast given by Theseus before the
tournament:

> The minstralcye, the service at the feeste,
> The grete yiftes to the meeste and leeste,
> The riche array of Theseus paleys,
> Ne who sat first ne last upon the deys,
> What ladies fairest been or best daunsinge,
> Or which of hem kan dauncen best and singe,
> Ne who moost felingly speketh of love;
> What haukes sitten on the perche above,
> What houndes liggen on the floor adoun—
> Of al this make I now no mencioun.   (1339–48)

Still more strikingly, it is used in the description of Arcite's
funeral in such a way that forty-six lines are spent in
mentioning what is *not* going to be described. The deception is transparent, and we are clearly intended to admire
the virtuosity with which the device is spun out. Such
virtuoso effects are the natural consequence of a concep-

tion of 'art' as technique, proficiency in which may be enjoyed for its own sake. 'The fascination of what's difficult' was strongly operative on medieval poets and their audiences, and their art of poetry tended to display rather than conceal itself. Similarly, in performances of ballet or opera today, the artists may be applauded for feats of physical or vocal athleticism, even though these are not strictly necessary at the point at which they occur.

The main part of the *artes poeticae* is concerned with amplifying rather than abbreviating one's material. The chief reason for this is no doubt that in the Middle Ages poetry was a pastime, as television is nowadays, and, in the absence of other forms of entertainment, the more time it could be expanded to fill, the better. Chaucer uses many of the amplifying devices recommended by the *artes poeticae*. Among these may be mentioned first the *exclamatio* or *apostrophatio*, in which the story is held up while a speech is addressed to some person or thing just mentioned or suggested by what has just been mentioned. (Characteristically it begins with an 'O!') Under this heading comes the narrator's comment at the point where Palamon and Arcite have arranged to meet next day to have a duel:

> O Cupide, out of alle charitee!
> O regne, that wolt no felawe have with thee!
> Ful sooth is seyd that love ne lordshipe
> Wol noght, his thankes, have no felaweshipe.
> Wel finden that Arcite and Palamoun.   (765–9)

In this example, the two *exclamationes* are followed by another common amplifying device, called *sententia*. This is a generalization about life, often based on a proverb, suggested by the particular event narrated in the story. *Sententiae* thus tend to begin with some such form of

words as 'Ful sooth is seyd that....' We might compare
this with an earlier example, when the narrator comments
that Palamon, hiding in the woods, would not have
expected to find Arcite there:

> God woot he wolde have trowed it ful lite.
> But sooth is seyd, go sithen many yeres,
> That 'feeld hath eyen and the wode hath eres.'
> It is ful fair a man to bere him evene,
> For al day meeteth men at unset stevene. (662–6)

Here two *sententiae* are juxtaposed. Another amplifying
device is the *exemplum*, which may be seen as the opposite
of the *sententia*. Where *sententia* supports a specific detail
in the narrative by a generalization, *exemplum* supports a
generalization with a particular example. Thus Theseus,
having digressed from the spectacle of Palamon and Arcite
fighting to the death for a lady who does not know of their
existence to say how powerful the god of love is, reverts
to their particular case as an *exemplum* illustrating Cupid's
power: Lo heere this Arcite and this Palamoun....   (933)

Again, the portraiture on the walls of the temple of Venus
is conceived as a series of *exempla* illustrating Venus's
power. The Knight lists various people who were depicted
there, draws the general moral, and then remarks that he
has only given a few of the thousand *ensamples* (i.e.
exempla) that prove its truth:

> Thus may ye seen that wisdom ne richesse,
> Beautee ne sleighte, strengthe ne hardinesse,
> Ne may with Venus holde champartie,
> For as hir list the world than may she gye.
> Lo, alle thise folk so caught were in hir las,
> Til they for wo ful ofte seyde 'allas!'
> Suffiseth heere ensamples oon or two,
> And though I koude rekene a thousand mo.
>
> (1089–96)

A further means of amplification is the *comparatio* or comparison. This is easily recognized:

> Ther nas no tigre in the vale of Galgopheye,
> Whan that hir whelp is stole whan it is lite,
> So crueel on the hunte as is Arcite
> For jelous herte upon this Palamon.   (1768–71)

Another, equally easy to recognize, is the *circumlocutio* or periphrasis. When Emelye goes to pray to Diana, she does not begin 'O Diana', but with a series of periphrases meaning the same thing:

> O chaste goddesse of the wodes grene,
> To whom bothe hevene and erthe and see is sene,
> Queene of the regne of Pluto derk and lowe,
> Goddesse of maidens....   (1439–42)

Descriptions

Finally we may mention the commonest device of all in *The Knight's Tale*, *descriptio* or description, of which I have already mentioned some prominent examples. Some of the *artes poeticae* are devoted almost entirely to description: a modern scholar has written of one of them (the *Ars Versificatoria* of Mathieu de Vendôme), 'His book seeks to further the writing of Latin descriptive verse. The idea behind it is that poetry is mainly description....'[1] A great deal of medieval poetry consists of description, and aims to offer a verbal equivalent for the visual arts of painting and tapestry. It is significant that in *The Knight's Tale* the descriptions of the three temples are descriptions of what was displayed on the walls in pictorial form. And this verbal description tends to follow the method of pictorial art in the Middle Ages, in enumerating detail in

[1] C. S. Baldwin, *Medieval Rhetoric and Poetic* (New York, 1928), p. 186.

an almost encyclopaedic way, rather than selecting a few salient details which will suggest the total impression. In pictorial art this mass of detail may be organized spatially so as to combine to form a single total effect; in verbal art, however, the detail can only be enumerated, and the result of this may be confusion and monotony. But in *The Knight's Tale* this danger is usually avoided, by making the descriptions convey not merely pictorial effects but certain ideas, which themselves act as organizing elements in the pictorial detail. It cannot be said that this technique was learned by Chaucer from the *artes poeticae*, because they have little to say about the *use* of descriptions. Geoffroi de Vinsauf writes simply: 'Descriptions spread out one's material. For when one has to make the brief statement that "Such a woman is beautiful", if a description of her beauty is given, then the brevity will be expanded.' Clearly he thinks of amplification as an end to be pursued for its own sake. The technique of using descriptions to convey ideas comes not from the *artes poeticae* but from what Chaucer makes of their doctrine through his own genius.

What his technique involves in *The Knight's Tale* can best be seen by examining a particular example in detail: the scene in which Emelye goes out to gather flowers in the garden in Maytime (175–221). This will involve some recapitulation of remarks made earlier. Now descriptions of spring and descriptions of beautiful girls are prescribed in the *artes poeticae* and fully supplied in the poetry based on them. In both cases, every detail of the description is laid down by tradition. In descriptions of spring we find bright sunshine, blue skies, flowers of various colours and kinds, birds singing, and so on, while the girl always has fair hair, grey eyes, a high forehead, graceful movements, and so on. What Chaucer has done is not simply to go through these conventional hoops, but to abbreviate both descriptions and run them together, so that the girl and the season become different aspects of a single complex idea. This idea cannot be simply stated, for it is uniquely created by this very passage, but it includes renewal, youth, vigour, and grace. The girl is compared with and vies with the spring flowers; her clothing is 'fressh', like the morning and the flowers; she rises as the sun rises; she gathers flowers with which to adorn her own head; she sings as the birds usually sing in the conventional spring-description. The girl becomes a personification of the season and the place; the season and the place become extensions of herself. Thus the description is unified and organized with a unique life. But this is not all. Having established the unity of girl and season, Chaucer goes on to juxtapose a description of a quite different kind:

> The grete tour, that was so thikke and stroong,
> Which of the castel was the chief dongeoun
> (Ther as the knightes weren in prisoun
> Of which I tolde yow and tellen shal)
> Was evene joinant to the gardyn wal
> Ther as this Emelye hadde hir pleyinge. (198–203)

The tower and the garden are next to each other, in the verse as in their physical location. The contrast intensifies the effect of each, and we are made to feel that both are part of the same world. The sequence of the description intertwines them, for next we see the girl and the garden again, through the eyes of Palamon in the tower,

> In which he al the noble citee seigh,
> And eek the gardyn, ful of braunches grene,
> Ther as this fresshe Emelye the shene
> Was in hire walk, and romed up and doun. (208–11)

40

Then we return to the tower itself, its harsh massiveness being powerfully evoked in the very sound of consonant-clusters through which the tongue must force its way with difficulty:

> That thurgh a window, thikke of many a barre
> Of iren greet and square as any sparre,
> He cast his eye upon Emelya.   (217–19)

Here the paradox of the union of garden and tower is particularly striking, since the massiveness of the tower is felt most fully in the description of the window through which Palamon sees Emelye in the garden. The garden and the tower are both symbolic features of the courtly life, and the total effect of this interlocking description is to suggest that in this life (and in the general human life of which it is a specialized and idealized version) opposite extremes of experience are violently yoked together. In this, as we shall see, the description is a small-scale representation of the effect of the whole Tale.

A similar descriptive technique is used throughout *The Knight's Tale*, but it is particularly noticeable in Part III, which consists almost entirely of descriptions. If we were expecting the action to bear the chief burden of the poem's meaning, we should no doubt expect this book to be the least relevant, the most extraneous and merely decorative. But the opposite is the case. *The Knight's Tale* is a poem in which the description gives meaning to the action, and so Part III becomes the core of the work's meaning. We shall be examining the nature of this meaning in a later part of this Introduction.

Descriptions of Action

This, however, will be a convenient place to say something of descriptions of a rather different kind—those of action. Most of the poem's descriptions are of people or places; hence they are lacking in physical movement, and the development that occurs in them is a development of ideas. But the poem also includes a number of descriptions of violent physical action, particularly in connexion with the tournament in Part IV, and these are strikingly successful in a quite different way from the static descriptions. They employ the same basic technique of the accumulation of details, but their success depends not on the unifying of details by a single dominant idea, but on the manipulation of the action itself. The descriptive technique used here is similar in some ways to that of the film. The poet's eye moves like the camera, giving the sense of bustling activity by switching rapidly from one shot to another, and pausing every so often to give a close-up of some especially significant or characteristic detail. In the description of the busy scene before the tournament (1633–64), an atmosphere of breathless haste is conveyed by the running on of the sense from one line to another and from one couplet to another:

> Knightes of retenue, and eek squieres
> Nailinge the speres....
> The fomy steedes on the golden bridel
> Gnawinge....   (1644–5, 1648–9)

At the same time, between two distant shots of people on horseback, a *ther maystow seen* in line 1638 draws us in for a close-up of richly decorated armour and equipment; and then the camera's eye, which has been ranging over the whole city, focuses on the random and busily talking groups in the palace, and we move among them, hearing snatches of their gossip. In the description of the tournament itself (1743–77), alliteration is used very heavily, to communicate directly the noise and impetus of battle. Chaucer here is not following exactly the structure of the alliterative verse which was being written in the north and west of England in his own time, but he did know of this verse (he makes the Parson refer to it, saying 'I kan nat geeste "rum, ram, ruf" by lettre') and no doubt recognized its special gift for conveying martial noise and movement. Again the effect is cinematic, mingling general views of the field (catching for instance the flash of silver as the swords are drawn), with rapidly successive shots of particular incidents, and finally coming to rest in formal descriptions of the two champions.

POETRY FOR READING ALOUD

We have seen that the virtuosity of the poem's technique might be displayed openly and admired for itself. The 'openness' of technique is partly a result of the conditions in which medieval poems were 'published'. For us, publication means the sending out to bookshops of printed copies of a work, to be bought by individual readers, each of whom will take the book home and read it privately. The reader will be able to go through a page as fast or as slowly as he thinks it demands, to turn back to look up something he has forgotten, to re-read the whole work and compare one part of it with another. But, as was suggested earlier in this Introduction, *The Knight's Tale*, at least in its earlier form as *Palamon and Arcite*, was probably 'published' by being read aloud, perhaps by the poet himself, to a small circle of courtly listeners, who would not possess their own copies of the work. Such conditions would demand a narrative method different in many respects from that usually employed in our own age. Not only the more virtuoso elements of literary technique would be 'open', but the very organization of the narrative would have to be done openly if the listeners were to be able to follow it. The poet will need to tell us explicitly that he is moving from one narrative thread to another, and this is particularly necessary with *The Knight's Tale*, where different parts of the story take place simultaneously in different countries. Thus, after Arcite has been banished from Athens, and Chaucer has repeated Palamon's speech bewailing his own situation, he conducts a transition from Palamon in Athens to Arcite in Thebes as follows:

> Now wol I stynte of Palamon a lite,
> And lete him in his prisoun stille dwelle,
> And of Arcita forth I wol yow telle.   (476–8)

Later in the poem, he wishes to leave Palamon and Arcite fighting their duel to explain that Theseus was hunting in the same wood, and he makes this transition equally explicit:

> And in this wise I lete hem fighting dwelle,
> And forth I wole of Theseus yow telle.   (803–4)

Open transitions may also be used simply to bracket a digression which interrupts the narrative line only briefly. At the very beginning of the Tale, we are told of Theseus's triumphant homecoming. The narrator then inserts the *occupatio* mentioned earlier, in which he remarks that he has no time to tell us of Theseus's victory and wedding feast, and afterwards returns to the homecoming. Now although this *occupatio* is a means of abbreviation, it is so positioned as to be a digression interrupting the narrative, and so it is prefaced with one transition—

> And thus with victorie and with melodye
> Lete I this noble duc to Atthenes ride,
> And al his hoost in armes him biside.
> And certes, if it nere to long to heere...   (14–17)

—and concluded by another—

> And ther I lefte, I wol ayeyn biginne.
> This duc of whom I make mencioun....   (34–5)

Another result of the fact that the poem was written for a listening audience is that this audience is itself directly addressed by the narrator. We have seen an example of this in the *demande d'amour* at the end of Part 1:

> Yow loveres axe I now this questioun:
> Who hath the worse, Arcite or Palamoun?
> (489–90)

Another occurs when the narrator passes over the feast before the tournament with an *occupatio*, and then uses this as a means of calling special attention to the prayers in the temples which come next:

> Of al this make I now no mencioun,
> But al th'effect, that thinketh me the beste.
> Now cometh the point, and herkneth if yow leste.
> (1348–50)

Again, before the appearance of the *furie infernal* to frighten Arcite's horse, we are warned to attend carefully with:

> But herkneth me, and stynteth noise a lite,
> Which a miracle ther bifel anon.   (1816–17)

We may take such remarks in *The Knight's Tale* as addressed to the other pilgrims, but demands for attention are extremely common in medieval poetry generally, though perhaps more common in poems recited to miscellaneous audiences by wandering minstrels than in courtly entertainments such as *Palamon and Arcite*.

One last result of oral delivery, which is to be found throughout the style of the poem, is the use of phrases which are little more than space-fillers. Thus in the following lines—

> And of the grete bataille for the nones
> Bitwixen Atthenes and Amazones   (21-2)

—the phrase *for the nones* would have to be translated by some such word as 'particularly', but in fact possesses scarcely any real meaning. It is employed partly for the rhyme with the unusual word *Amazones* and partly to give the listeners time to catch up. When we are told of Theseus 'No neer Atthenes wolde he go ne ride' (110), the phrase *go ne ride* does not imply any real distinction between going on foot and going on horseback; it is simply an emphatic way of saying 'go'. Similarly, in the line 'And so bifel, by aventure or cas' (216), *aventure* and *cas* are not really alternatives—indeed they mean exactly the same —but simply give a certain emphasis to the idea of chance. The style of a poem intended to be read aloud cannot afford to be too concentrated. It needs to contain a certain proportion of familiar formulas which demand no attention either for their meaning or for their novelty of phrasing. In *The Knight's Tale* many of these formulas serve a second purpose at the same time, by adding to the superlative quality of the poem's world. Thus we find many phrases that include or exclude everything by mentioning two extremes of some kind: *bothe lasse and moore* meaning 'all' (898); *hoot and coold* meaning 'everything' (953); *night ne day* meaning 'at any time' (965); *alle and some* meaning 'all' (1329); *where I ride or go* meaning 'at all times' (1394; compare 110 quoted above); and many others. Such phrases could be justified according to the *ars poetica* as examples of *circumlocution*, but they are also natural parts of the idiom of orally delivered poetry.

THE KNIGHT AND HIS TALE

What has been offered so far in this Introduction has been largely information rather than interpretation, and has been intended to help modern readers to recognize and understand the *kind* of poem that *The Knight's Tale* is, and particularly how different it is from more modern kinds of literature. I now wish to try to suggest something of the significance of this poem as a work of literature—a more controversial matter, on which disagreement is to be expected. We have so far been considering *The Knight's Tale* mainly not as one of *The Canterbury Tales* but as the separate work referred to in the Prologue to *The Legend of Good Women* as 'the love of Palamon and Arcite'. We do not know what changes Chaucer may have made in this separate work when he included it in *The Canterbury Tales*; but even if he did not alter a word, 'the love of Palamon and Arcite' was inevitably transformed into a different poem when it became *The Knight's Tale*. The effect on any tale of giving it a fictional teller and setting it in the context of a pilgrimage where the other pilgrims also tell tales of quite different kinds will be to place it in an entirely new perspective. It will become not Chaucer's story but its teller's story: a teller whose attitude towards his tale and towards life is not necessarily that of the author, especially since that author is himself presented as one of the pilgrims. We shall be encouraged in such a situation not simply to accept the tale, but to judge it. This is most obviously and crudely the case when we come to the second tale of the pilgrimage, which is told by the Miller, and takes the form of a bawdy parody of *The Knight's Tale*, reproducing the same human situation as farce instead of chivalric romance. Such a relationship is characteristic of *The Canterbury Tales*, a work whose basic conception is of the variety of life and of the possible attitudes towards it. But even within *The Knight's Tale* alone, we seem to detect a point of view which belongs to the Knight and which is not the only point of view possible. The Knight is described in *The General Prologue* as an idealized and composite figure,[1] rather than a unique individual like the Pardoner or the Wife of Bath. Yet, for all his ideal quality, he is also noticeably an old-fashioned figure. He is elderly, somewhat shabby: the ideals by which he has lived in his crusading life are noble but innocent. He scarcely seems to belong to the world inhabited by the majority of the pilgrims, the 'newe world' mentioned in connexion with the worldly Monk, a world devoted not to an ideal of service but to power, to acquisition, to self-assertion. And a certain innocence is detectable in his own attitude towards the tale he tells. This is most strikingly apparent in one of his own comments on his story. Having described the great flocking of knights to the tournament, and said how glad those were who were chosen to take part in it, he goes on:

> For if ther fille tomorwe swich a cas,
> Ye knowen wel that every lusty knight
> That loveth paramours and hath his might,

[1] See pp. 191–2 of this edition.

Were it in Engelond or elleswhere,
They wolde, hir thankes, wilnen to be there—
To fighte for a lady, *benedicitee*,
It were a lusty sighte for to see.   (1252–8)

The world of the Tale, though it certainly reflects the
aspirations or fantasies of the aristocracy, is not so easily
to be identified with 'Engelond' and 'tomorwe'—there is
indeed some evidence that Richard II was more eager to
hold tournaments than the aristocracy were to take part in
them. We cannot help feeling that the Knight's enthusiasm, though touching, is ingenuous. This is only a single
detail; but in general, when we think of the Tale as being
the Knight's, we begin to see it in a new light. It is not
that the Tale itself comes to seem limited by the Knight's
own innocence of attitude, but rather that *we* are able to
see more in it than he can see. He is enthusiastically inside
it; we are outside it, and from our more detached view-
point can recognize a sombreness that he is scarcely aware
of. The whole poem is governed by a convention of super-
latives and extremes; everything in it is the best or worst
of its kind. When we see it as a tale told by the Knight,
these appear as an expression of his own idealism and
enthusiasm. But, as a result of this new perspective, we
can recognize that they also have a meaning that he does
not see. For they are the means by which the very texture
of the Tale supports and expands a view of life implied
by its story—of life as a matter of violent contrasts between opposite extremes of fortune, between prosperity
and disaster. This vision of life is already outlined in the
opening incident of the poem, where the widows draw a
contrast between their misery and Theseus's triumph, and
again between their past glory and their present wretched-

ness. Similar contrasts run throughout the poem: between Theseus's lifelong happiness and Palamon and Arcite's lifelong imprisonment—

> He took his hoost, and hoom he rit anon
> With laurer crowned as a conquerour;
> And ther he liveth in joye and in honour
> Terme of his lyf; what nedeth wordes mo?
> And in a tour, in angwissh and in wo,
> This Palamon and his felawe Arcite
> For everemoore; ther may no gold hem quite
>
> (168–74)

—between the castle-prison and the garden adjoining it (a contrast we have already seen expanded in interlocking descriptions); between Arcite's freedom and rise in Theseus's service and Palamon's continued imprisonment—

> Ther was no man that Theseus hath derre.
> And in this blisse lete I now Arcite,
> And speke I wole of Palamon a lite.
> In derknesse and horrible and strong prisoun
> Thise seven yeer hath seten Palamoun
> Forpined, what for wo and for distresse   (590–5)

—between Arcite's happiness as he sings the roundel and his sudden fit of melancholy; between his former royal state and his new position as a squire; between the two knights' friendship in arming each other and their savagery in the duel; between Arcite's victory in the tournament and his sudden downfall. Pervasively, to an extent which we realize all the more fully because the Knight himself does not seem to realize it, but only to see the superlative and astonishing, the Tale conveys a sense of human life as full of contrast, veering violently and uncontrollably from one extreme to another. It is a vision of life summed up with piercing economy by Arcite in his dying speech, in the contrast between the warm companionship of love and the cold solitude of the grave:

> What is this world? what asketh men to have?
> Now with his love, now in his colde grave
> Allone, withouten any compaignye. (1919-21)

It is towards this kind of insight into the nature of the general human condition that the Tale drives, and this is why it is not necessary that we should be interested in the characters as individuals. They are men, and men, according to the view of life embodied in the Tale, are forced by their common destiny into a unity more important than the accidental differences of character. It is a poem about life in general, a philosophical poem.

FORTUNE

It is philosophical in an explicit way, not merely by implication. The vision of life as a matter of violent contrasts and changes is not merely embodied in the action of the Tale, but is conceptualized, particularly in the earlier part of the poem, under the name of Fortune. Thus in that opening incident to which we have several times reverted as a paradigm of the whole poem, the eldest widow first addresses Theseus as

> ...Lord, to whom *Fortune* hath yiven
> Victorie, and as a conqueror to liven, (57-8)

and then, having said that all the ladies were once royal or noble, adds

> Now be we caytyves, as it is wel seene,
> Thanked be *Fortune* and her false wheel,
> That noon estaat assureth to be weel. (66-8)

Arcite, thinking that Palamon's cry is one of anguish at their imprisonment, tells him to be patient because

> *Fortune* hath yeven us this adversitee. (228)

When Arcite has been freed, he envies Palamon's lot, saying

> Wel hath *Fortune* yturned thee the dys. (380)

And when Theseus arranges the tournament to decide whom Emelye shall marry, he is aware of placing the choice in the hands of Fortune—

> ...Thanne shal I yeve Emelya to wyve
> To whom that *Fortune* yeveth so fair a grace.
>
> (1002–3)

Fortune, like so much else in *The Knight's Tale*, is a characteristically medieval idea. In one sense, we all know what Fortune means—it is chance, what 'just happens', without any human intention being operative. But, for the Middle Ages, Fortune had a much greater hold on the imagination than it does today. People then were much more conscious than most of us are nowadays of the insecurity of human life and of the dramatic changes which may come upon any man unawares. They felt this so strongly that they conceived of Fortune as a personal force, and imagined it as a woman with an incessantly turning wheel, to whose revolutions all humanity was subject. This is what the widow means by

> ...Fortune and her false wheel,
> That noon estaat assureth to be weel.

Every condition of life is unstable; no one, however high his position, can be sure that it will continue, and indeed, as the wheel image suggests, the higher the position, the more likely is a sudden descent. One important source of this conception of Fortune, which we find everywhere in medieval thought about the human condition, is a work by a fifth-century Roman philosopher, the *De Consolatione Philosophiae* of Boethius. Boethius had been a high statesman, but he was then suddenly sent to prison (where he was eventually tortured and executed). The book was written after his imprisonment, and it tells how he is visited in prison by Philosophy herself, in the form of a beautiful and terrifying lady. In an extended dialogue with her, he is cured of a rebellious attitude of mind towards his misfortunes, and is brought to accept them with a new understanding. Book II of the *De Consolatione* is concerned chiefly with Fortune. Philosophy presents the whole world as governed by Fortune, but denies that what happens to men in their subjection to her is to be interpreted as reward or punishment. In herself, Fortune is a non-moral force, and she does not bring men to prosperity for their virtues or to disgrace (like Boethius's) for their sins; that is simply what the world is like. Now Boethius was one of Chaucer's own favourite philosophers. Somewhere around the date of *Palamon and Arcite* he had written a complete English translation of the *De Consolatione*, and *The Knight's Tale* is full of verbal echoes of it and arguments taken from it. None of these is to be found in the *Teseida*. There can be no doubt that in *The Knight's Tale* Chaucer presents a world similar to that described by Philosophy in Book II of the *De Consolatione*, a world in which the only certainty is that things will change, for (to quote from Chaucer's translation) 'It is certeyn and established by lawe perdurable that nothing that is engendred nis stedfast ne stable'. In this world people do not get what they deserve—it cannot possibly be said that on moral grounds Arcite deserves to die, or

Palamon deserves to get Emelye. Human nobility is not rewarded by success, but, on the contrary, is most fully shown in response to undeserved adversity. Hence the moving quality of Arcite's dying speech, in which he shows a generosity foreign to the force by which he has been killed.

THE GODS

It cannot be said, however, that Arcite has been killed directly by Fortune. He is not shown, as he might easily be in a medieval poem, as being cast down from the highest point on her wheel, but as being killed when a 'furie infernal' sent by Saturn frightens his horse and causes it to throw him. The references to Fortune are chiefly in the first half of *The Knight's Tale*, and as the story progresses the force by which the human events of the poem are controlled is realized more distinctly and more variously as consisting of a number of gods. The first of these to be mentioned is the one who is eventually responsible for Arcite's death, Saturn. He is mentioned as an alternative to or explanation of a reference to Fortune. When Arcite tells Palamon not to cry out in anguish at their imprisonment 'for it may noon oother be', he goes on:

> Fortune hath yeven us this adversitee.
> Som wikke aspect or disposicioun
> Of Saturne, by som constellacioun,
> Hath yeven us this, although we hadde it sworn;
> So stood the hevene whan that we were born.
>
> (228–32)

Next we hear of a goddess, Venus, when Palamon wonders whether Emelye is Venus, and prays to her (243–7). Palamon at the end of Part I laments that he is in prison because of Saturn, and also because of another goddess,

Juno, who is offended with the Thebans, while on the other hand he is tormented with jealousy caused by Venus (470–5). It is from another god, Mercury, whom he sees in a dream, that Arcite gets the idea of returning to Athens (527–34). It is Venus who changes Arcite's joy into melancholy, in the same way as she causes changes in the weather of her day, Friday (676–81). He apostrophizes Mars and Venus as causers of his family's fall from prosperity (just the kind of event that is elsewhere attributed to Fortune). We are told of Theseus when he goes hunting that 'after Mars he serveth now Diane' (824). But it is in Part III that the gods really take control, both of the action and of the poetry. First we have the long descriptions of the three temples of Venus, Mars, and Diana; then the prayers in each of them, and the responses received; then, for the first time, we are taken among the gods themselves. We see the quarrel between Mars and Venus and its settlement by Saturn, who defines his own nature in a long speech. After this, we are returned from the heavens to see Saturn's decision worked out on earth, in the intervention of the 'furie' which kills Arcite after he has gained the victory, and thus allows both Mars and Venus to keep their promises to their devotees. The great and increasing importance of the gods as motivating forces in the story is obvious. We must now ask who or what these gods are.

The functions of the gods and medieval astrology

Their names are those of the gods of Roman paganism. The story of the poem is supposed to be set in ancient Greece, but these gods are still appropriate, for there was a close correspondence between Greek and Roman mythology, and in the Middle Ages, when Greek was little known in Western Europe, the Greek gods were usually called by their Roman names. It may be useful to insert here a brief account of who the gods mentioned in the poem were, information which can easily be skipped by those to whom it is already familiar.

Jupiter was the father and king of the gods. His father was *Saturn*, whom he had deposed, but who remains a potent force in mythology, and especially in this poem. Jupiter's wife was *Juno*. Among the other chief deities are *Mercury*, the messenger of the gods, with whom oracles were associated, and who was also the god of sleep and dreams; *Mars*, the god of war; *Venus*, the goddess of love, whose husband was *Vulcan*, the smith of the gods, and whose son was *Cupid*, the god of courtly love in the Middle Ages; *Pluto*, the god of the underworld; and *Diana*, the goddess of the moon, of hunting, of chastity, and of childbirth. Various fables concerning the relations of these gods with each other and with certain mortals are alluded to here and there in *The Knight's Tale*, and are explained at the appropriate point in the notes.

Chaucer would have learned about the special powers of the gods, and the emblems associated with them, not only from classical Latin literature but also from medieval encyclopaedias of mythology. Two of these that he may have read are the *De Deorum Imaginibus* of Albericus and Boccaccio's *De Genealogia Deorum*.

Chaucer shows an accurate knowledge of this mythology, but, as we have seen, there is very little historical interest in *The Knight's Tale*, and it can scarcely be included in the interests of mere antiquarian accuracy. The fact is that the pagan gods survived into Chaucer's own time, but they did so in a surprising form. In ancient times, the seven planets that were then known (among which were included the sun and the moon) had been given the names of gods: Mercury, Venus, Mars, Jupiter, Saturn, Diana (or Luna, the moon), and Phoebus Apollo (or Sol, the sun).[1] Now in the Middle Ages there was widespread belief in the 'science' of astrology, according to which the heavenly bodies, and especially the planets, had a direct effect on human life. The characters and fates of individuals were influenced by the relationship of the stars at their birth—this is what Arcite is referring to when he tells Palamon 'So stood the hevene whan that we were born' (232). Moreover, certain planets were dominant in certain periods and at certain times of day, and were then able to influence human life in general.[2] It was thus perfectly possible for medieval people to go on believing in the power of the pagan gods (about whom they read so much in the Latin literature on which medieval education was chiefly based), while at the same time believing in Christianity. The medieval Church did not deny that the planets influenced human life, only that they exercised a determining influence, which would exclude human free will. But the precise extent to which the planetary gods governed men's lives was probably a matter which most non-theologians did not bother to define: they could comfortably believe simultaneously in the gods and in God.

[1] Apollo was the god of healing and of music and poetry. He is mentioned in *The Knight's Tale* only as 'firy Phebus' (635), meaning simply the sun.

[2] A more detailed account of medieval astrology is given in *An Introduction to Chaucer*, pp. 163–76.

The temples of the gods

There can be no doubt that Chaucer himself was deeply
interested both in astrology and in the astronomy on which
it was based. He wrote one prose work on astronomy
himself (*The Treatise on the Astrolabe*), and may have
written another (*The Equatorie of the Planetis*). He found
in the *Teseida* a story in which the gods already played a
considerable part, and in translating it he brought them
into even more striking prominence, and made them more
completely responsible for the action of the story. It was
Chaucer, for example, who introduced the vision of
Mercury by which Arcite was persuaded to return to
Athens. But his bringing of the gods into prominence
and his identification of the gods with the planets are most
apparent in Part III, and we must now turn to examine
this in more detail.

The descriptions of the three temples of Venus, Mars,
and Diana are used by Chaucer to convey thought about
the meaning of the gods. For him this meaning is both
more important and more sombre than it was for Boccaccio. In the description of the temple of Venus (1060–
108), the opening lines, with their generalizing list of the
sufferings 'That loves servantz in this lyf enduren', are a
Chaucerian addition. Then comes a list of personifications connected with love, where good and bad qualities
are mingled in utter disorder, for Venus has nothing to
do with moral virtue. Next there is a description of
Venus's dwelling, which gradually merges into the garden
of love as depicted in the *Roman de la Rose*, and this in
turn merges into a list of well-known legendary figures
who suffered through love. Here particularly, if we are

to make any sense at all of the description, it is necessary to interpret its meaning intellectually rather than rely on an instinctive response to its decorative quality (which indeed is scarcely noticeable). Narcissus died through falling in love with his own reflexion in a pool; Solomon was led into idolatry by his wives and concubines; Hercules was killed by a poisoned shirt sent him by his wife out of jealousy (jealousy has been among the list of personifications); Medea murdered her own children; Circe turned men into animals; Turnus was killed fighting for the love of Lavinia. What is illustrated by this list is not simply the universal power of Venus, but the fact that this power is destructive and brings men to miserable ends. And this point is made more explicitly at the end, in some lines that were also added by Chaucer:

> Lo, alle thise folk so caught were in hir las,
> Til they for wo ful ofte seyde 'allas!'   (1093–4)

Finally comes the statue of Venus herself, full of appeal to the senses and surrounded by the traditional emblems listed by medieval writers on mythology; but here too there is a suggestion of the destructive, for she is accompanied by her son Cupid armed with 'arwes brighte and kene'. Thus the force in human life that Venus represents —sexual love—is very fully defined in this description: alluring, all-powerful, morally neutral, and destructive.

The description of the temple of Mars (1109–92) similarly functions as a statement of the nature of the force Mars represents. What this force is, is best conveyed by the memorable poetry of the description itself, rather than by any abstract definition. It may be roughly summed up as violence, and, more noticeably than in the Venus description, Mars must be seen simultaneously as

the god of war (who stands for human aggressive impulses)
and as the planet (which causes wars and other displays of
violence on earth). The description begins less abstractly
than that of the temple of Venus, by evoking the atmosphere of 'the grete temple of Mars in Trace', which is
painted on the wall. The dead forest rocked by the wind,
the effect of which is conveyed through the alliterative
harshness and difficulty of the actual sound—

> With knotty, knarry, bareyne trees olde,
> Of stubbes sharpe and hidouse to biholde,
> In which ther ran a rumbel in a swough,
> As though a storm sholde bresten every bough
> (1119–22)

—the glitter of steel, the frightening noises, the cold dim
light, the brutal strength of the iron reinforcing the doors
and the pillars: all this offers an unforgettable *poetic*
definition of heartless violence. There follows a survey of
the operations of Mars in the actual world, in which per-
sonified abstractions are jumbled together with typical
persons and scenes, so that Fear and a pickpocket jostle
in the same line. Many of the items in this list are horribly
memorable in themselves: the vignette of the suicide
bathed in his own blood—

> The sleere of himself yet saugh I ther—
> His herte-blood hath bathed al his heer (1147–8)

—or the justly famous line in which the essentials of
treachery are collected with the utmost economy:

> The smilere with the knyf under the cloke. (1141)

The total effect of the list, mixing allegory with genre-
painting, and putting the abstract Conquest in place of
the individual Damocles—

> And al above, depeynted in a tour,
> Saugh I Conquest sittinge in greet honour,
> With the sharpe swerd over his heed
> Hanginge by a soutil twines threed   (1169–72)

—is to make us feel the abstractions at work in everyday
life, not merely in their own special world. The influence
of Mars is felt in all nations and all classes—Julius Caesar
rubs shoulders with the cook and the pickpocket—and his
power shows itself as much in the squalid accidents of
everyday life as in world-historical events. Finally comes
the statue of Mars himself, surrounded like that of Venus
by his traditional emblems, here the chariot and the man-
eating wolf (the last detail being added by Chaucer).

The third temple description, that of Diana (1193–230),
is entirely a Chaucerian addition, but its method is
exactly the same as the others, a definition by extension
of the force in human life represented by the planet-
goddess. What this force is is considerably more difficult
to say than in the case of Mars or Venus. The complex
of ideas and feelings represented by Diana is no longer
perceived in our time as a unity, and we have no word to
express it. Chaucer himself sums up the description as
being 'Of hunting and of shamefast chastitee', Diana being
goddess of both. The connexion between her two roles
(as we have seen, she has others too) seems to us fortuitous,
but was perhaps not felt to be so in the Middle Ages. She
seems to stand for chastity conceived ambivalently, both
as holy and as a potentially destructive refusal of the
deepest human relationship. In the temple description, at
any rate, Diana is seen, like Venus and Mars, as a force
whose power is directed towards destruction. Chaucer
gives a list of the victims of Diana compiled from Ovid's

Metamorphoses: Callisto transformed into a bear, Daphne into a laurel tree, Actaeon into a stag which was then killed by his own hounds, and so on. Then follows the usual description of the goddess's statue, containing emblematic allusions to her connexions with the fickle moon, with the sinister underworld, and with the pain of childbirth.

The conflict of the gods and Saturn's solution

These then are the forces by which the world of *The Knight's Tale* is immediately governed, and they are defined by the descriptions in Part III as universally powerful and universally destructive. But the course of the story now brings these forces into conflict among themselves. Palamon prays to Venus for possession of Emelye, and Arcite prays to Mars for victory in the tournament which is to determine possession of her, and both their prayers are granted. The result, naturally, is strife in heaven between Venus and Mars, since they appear to have promised incompatible things (or, if we think of it in astrological terms, to have predicted incompatible futures). In the *Teseida* this strife is settled by an ingenious device, the origin of which is not specified. But Chaucer, with greater consistency, continues the astrological motivation. First of all Jupiter, the father of the gods, attempts to put an end to the quarrel, but he has no success. Saturn, the father of Jupiter, and oldest of the gods, takes his place, and

> Foond in his olde experience an art
> That he ful soone hath plesed every part.

> (1587–8)

In doing so, he makes a speech which is in effect a definition of his own nature, and thus provides a parallel to the
three earlier temple descriptions. It works in the same
way as these descriptions, and particularly that of Mars,
in asserting the universality of the god's power by juxta-
posing a variety of examples of its effect. But the power
assigned to Saturn by medieval astrology was not so much,
like that of the other three, over human impulses, as over
the external conditions of human life. Saturn is the force
that produces disasters, and he lists them in his speech—
drowning, imprisonment, strangling, rebellion, the collapse of buildings, plague. The speech is magnificently
sombre, organized by a rhetoric that constantly returns to
an assertion of personal power:

> *Myn is* the drenching in the see so wan;
> *Myn is* the prison in the derke cote;
> *Myn is* the strangling and hanging by the throte,
> The murmure and the cherles rebelling.... (1598–601)

Moreover, its different details are unified by having applied
to them adjectives that express the nature of Saturn himself, as conceived by medieval astrology. He is responsible
for 'the drenching in the see so *wan*', for 'the prison in the
derke cote', for 'the maladies *colde*', for 'the *derke* tresons,
and the castes *olde*'. All these adjectives stand for attributes of the planet-god himself. Chaucer has made the
ponderous symmetries of Part III point towards the oldest
and most inimical of the seven planetary gods—*Infortuna
major*, as he was called by the astrologers. This is the
arbitrating force in the poem's universe, a force that
crushes mankind beneath inexplicable disasters. And the
solution he finds to the conflict between Mars and Venus
is in keeping with his nature as defined in this speech.

He first allows Arcite to be victorious in the tournament, so that Mars may carry out his promise. Venus thinks she is shamed—

> What seith she now? What dooth this queene of love,
> But wepeth so, for wantinge of hir wille,
> Til that hir teeres in the listes fille?   (1806–8)

—but Saturn replies, 'Doghter, hoold thy pees', and then sends the 'furie infernal' which startles Arcite's horse and causes him to be fatally injured. Thus Palamon may eventually possess Emelye, and Venus's promise too can be carried out. But this solution is of course utterly callous of human suffering, and we are not allowed to disregard the suffering it involves. The death agony of Arcite is described in the fullest possible medical detail, including the 'clothered blood', the swelling of 'the pipes of his longes', and the accumulation of 'venym and corrupcioun' in his chest. Significantly, most of this detail, which is completely accurate in terms of medieval medicine, was added by Chaucer, and there can be no doubt, I think, that his purpose was to fix our attention on the horror of Arcite's death, rather than to allow it to rest complacently on the ingenious solution chosen by Saturn. The contrast between human suffering and divine callousness is striking, and a similar contrast seems to arise a little later, in Arcite's dying speech, between human generosity and divine pettiness. Arcite has been made to die in agony at the moment of his apparent triumph in order to settle a quarrel between gods who are presented as bickering like children (hence Saturn's blunt 'Doghter, hoold thy pees'). But he can rise above the squalid circumstances of his death to a final display of *gentillesse*, in recommending his rival to Emelye. Arcite is less powerful but more noble than the gods who have killed him, and thus the aristocratic value-system centring in *gentillesse* comes to have metaphysical implications. In order to discuss these, we shall have finally to consider the poem's explicit philosophizing; but before we do so, it will be worth returning to the main body of the poem to see how far the view of human life implied by the conception of the planetary gods runs through the work as a whole.

THE HUMAN CONDITION

[handwritten annotation: gods with human attributes]

We have seen that the gods as Chaucer conceives them and brings them into prominence in *The Knight's Tale* are not merely antiquarian accompaniments to an action set in the classical past. As well as being anthropomorphic deities with a personal life of a human kind, they are the planets of medieval astrology—powers which govern human behaviour. The mythology of the poem, like any significant mythology, is the imaginative expression of a conception of the nature of human life. The gods are, we may say, the conditions under which life itself is lived. Since human beings act partly from their own motives and partly from the effect of circumstances outside themselves, we may say that these conditions are partly internal and partly external. Of the four gods formally presented in Part III, Venus and Mars represent the impulses by which men in the world of the poem are motivated from within. Since the poem's milieu is chivalric, and thus human activity is presented in it as consisting mainly of love and war, these are naturally the erotic and aggressive impulses. Saturn represents the external conditions of human life; and in the world of the poem these appear as a bent towards disaster or misfortune.

The function of Diana, as we have seen, is more difficult for a modern reader to grasp; she seems to stand partly for a human impulse—the impulse of withdrawal from relationship—and partly for an external circumstance, a tendency towards destruction similar to that represented by Saturn. Diana is in any case the least dominant of the four gods. Thus between them, the planetary gods present an extremely pessimistic view of human life. Men, according to the poem's mythology, are enslaved both by their own passions and by the nature of the world they inhabit, and by both equally they are driven towards misery and death.

This view of life is not found only in the mythological superstructure erected in Part III. It is also found throughout the poem in non-mythological forms, and most noticeably in the poem's most characteristic imagery. There are two trains of imagery which run throughout *The Knight's Tale*, and which serve to reinforce its mythology. These are beast-images and prison-images, and they suggest that man is an animal, both in his uncontrollable passions and in his ignorant subjection to external forces, and that life itself is a prison. These images will be worth examining in some detail.

ANIMAL IMAGERY AND THE ROLE OF THESEUS

Animal images indicating ferocity are applied most strikingly to the two knights. Love, according to Arcite's speech on the subject after he and Palamon have both seen Emelye for the first time, is a force which overrides all laws and reduces man to a Hobbesian state of nature: 'Ech man for himself, ther is noon oother' (324). In the same

speech he imagines himself and Palamon as two dogs
fighting for a bone. And love does indeed release an
animal-like ferocity in the two. When they meet unexpectedly in Athens, they are immediately at each others'
throats, and Arcite 'as fiers as leon pulled out his swerd'
(740). They agree to meet next day on equal terms, but
the *gentillesse* of their conduct in helping to arm each other
only makes more striking the contrast between the civilized
surface and the animal passions beneath it. First we are
told that they are like hunters of the lion or bear waiting
for their prey to rush at them. Then three animal similes
follow in quick succession:

> Thou mightest wene that this Palamon
> In his fighting were a wood leon,
> And as a crueel tigre was Arcite;
> As wilde bores gonne they to smite,
> That frothen whit as foom for ire wood.
>
> (797–801)

When they are interrupted by Theseus, the last image is
repeated:

> He was war of Arcite and Palamon,
> That foughten breme as it were bores two.
>
> (840–1)

Theseus is out hunting when he comes upon them, and
here hunting seems to carry suggestions of the restraint
or ordering of the animal qualities. Theseus stands as an
opposite to all that the animal imagery implies about man.
He can control his own passions, and his aim is always
to moderate, to impose order on disorder: he turns the
illegal private duel into a ceremonial public act. But there
is perhaps a certain ambivalence in the idea of Theseus
as a hunter, in the light of the previous hunting image, in
which the hunter, engaged in a desperate battle for survival

with his prey, seemed as savage as it, and as reduced from
rational status. The savage aspect of hunting is emphasized in the conception of Diana as a huntress. A persistent irony follows Theseus, by which his attempts to
impose a civilized order on human life lead only to greater
destruction, clothed though this may be in chivalric
pageantry. This has been seen on a small scale in the
poem's first episode, where his generous response to the
widows' plea for mercy led to the total destruction of
the city of Thebes. He marched against Thebes with two
emblems: a banner showing an image of Mars (and we
have seen what Mars stands for), and his private pennon

> Of gold ful riche, in which ther was ybete
> The Minotaur, which that he slough in Crete.
>
> (121–2)

The Minotaur was a monster, half man and half bull, and
thus a perfect image of the bestial element in man. Theseus
had killed it, but now he carries it as his emblem, and it is
difficult to resist seeing in this a telling irony: Theseus is
himself an exponent of the very force he is proud of having
destroyed. The pattern is repeated in the main part of
the poem. Theseus first converts the private duel into a
public tournament, and then ordains that in the tournament no one shall be killed; but the result of all this is
that Arcite dies a horrible death. And the magnificent
pageantry of the tournament itself, which from one point
of view is the supreme expression of the civilized chivalric
order, in fact expresses, rather than conceals, the disorder
and savagery which the order is intended to govern.

The lists constructed by Theseus are in the form of an
amphitheatre, and their circular shape is itself the traditional symbol of order and perfection. Theseus, when he

constructs the amphitheatre, is like God creating the world by reducing chaos to order; and, just as God when the world was made saw that it was good, so we are told of Theseus that 'Whan it was doon, him liked wonder weel' (1234). The chief decorative features of the amphitheatre are the temples of Venus, Mars, and Diana, but these key-stones of the amphitheatre's ceremonial order themselves symbolize the very opposite: disruptive violence. The temple descriptions include much animal imagery. The power of Venus is exemplified by Circe, who transformed men into beasts. Mars has at his feet a wolf devouring a man. Diana is represented by a number of metamor-phoses, including those of the transformation of Callisto into a bear and of Actaeon into a stag. But the animal imagery culminates in another part of the pageantry, the processional appearance of the two champions, Lygurge and Emetreus. Both are terrifyingly like wild animals in appearance and trappings. Lygurge stares like a griffin, with eyes that 'gloweden bitwixen yelow and reed'. He wears a black bear-skin, complete with claws, and his hair shines 'as any ravenes fethere'. He rides in a chariot drawn by bulls and followed by dogs 'To hunten at the leoun or the deer.' Emetreus is compared first to Mars and then to a lion. He has an animal's yellowish-green eyes, carries an eagle on his wrist, and is followed by lions and leopards. Emetreus particularly is totally metamor-phosed into a wild beast, or rather into a composite symbol of the savage, and the two together make up a magnificent and terrifying image of the animal in man. When the tournament itself is reached, the beast images applied to the duel are repeated in a formalized and expanded form as epic similes:

> Ther nas no tigre in the vale of Galgopheye,
> Whan that hir whelp is stole whan it is lite,
> So crueel on the hunte as is Arcite
> For jelous herte upon this Palamon.
> Ne in Belmarye ther nis so fel leon,
> That hunted is, or for his hunger wood,
> Ne of his praye desireth so the blood,
> As Palamon to sleen his foo Arcite.   (1768–75)

Again hunting and savagery are connected.

Animal imagery of a different kind is also used to express the indignity or even absurdity of the human condition. At the end of Part I, Palamon has a philosophical speech in which he asks indignantly what meaning there is in the universe, and the backbone of the speech is a comparison between men and animals. He begins by asking the 'crueel goddes'

> What is mankinde moore unto you holde
> Than is the sheep that rouketh in the folde?
> For slain is man right as another beest.... (449-51)

He goes on to point out that the animals can satisfy their desires in life and suffer no pain after death, whereas men must deprive themselves in life and are then punished when they die. Men are in a worse position than animals. Before this, Arcite has said that we men, in our ignorance of what is good for us, go through life 'as he that dronke is as a mous' (403), and there too the animal image, though applied only obliquely, is degrading. Somewhat similarly, though with amusement rather than Palamon's indignation or Arcite's despair, Theseus points out that the two lovers are about to slaughter each other in their duel for Emelye, while

> She woot namoore of al this hoote fare,
> By God, than woot a cokkow or an hare!   (951-2)

Sheep, mouse, cuckoo, hare: such images debase the human condition by seeing it as absurd.

Introduction

PRISON IMAGERY

Prison imagery is used less often in *The Knight's Tale* than animal imagery, but because it is narrative rather than merely verbal, it has perhaps no less force. We have seen how powerfully the actual prison in which Palamon and Arcite are put for life is realized in the poem as a matter of walls and bars 'greet and square as any sparre'. Naturally their thoughts revert to it again and again, until imprisonment comes to seem an image of the human condition itself:

> For wel thou woost thyselven, verraily,
> That thou and I be dampned to prisoun
> Perpetuelly; us gaineth no raunsoun.   (316–18)

The idea of life as a prison from which men escape only by death is traditional both in Platonism and in Christianity, and it is a fundamental notion in the philosophical work which underlies so much of the poem's thought, the *De Consolatione*. There Boethius is in a physical prison, which eventually comes to seem an image of life itself. And in *The Knight's Tale*, in the long speech derived from Boethian philosophy with which Theseus attempts to expound the significance and moral of the poem's events, the same idea occurs when he argues

> That goode Arcite, of chivalrie the flour,
> Departed is with duetee and honour
> Out of this foule prisoun of this lyf.   (2201–3)

The phrasing is casual and unoriginal, but as it occurs in this final position in the poem, and after all the earlier references to an actual prison, it strikes home.

EXPLICIT PHILOSOPHY

Arcite

I have claimed that *The Knight's Tale* is a philosophical poem, and it is so not merely by implication but explicitly. It is characteristic of Chaucer's poetry, that when his characters find themselves in an extreme situation of some kind, they are not content to rejoice in their personal lot or to bewail it, but they are provoked to statements or questions about life in general. This is particularly the case with characters reduced to misery: they move outwards from lamentation to philosophical questioning. Thus in *Troilus and Criseyde*, when Troilus has his mistress torn away from him by an unwished-for exchange of prisoners, he embarks on a discussion of predestination and freewill. And in *The Franklin's Tale*, when Dorigen's husband leaves her to go across the sea in pursuit of martial adventure, she looks at the rocks on the coastline and asks in philosophical terms for what purpose a benevolent god could have created them. Similarly, in *The Knight's Tale*, at the end of Part I, when Arcite is released from prison but banished from Athens and Emelye, he does not merely comment on his own folly in having wished to escape from his prison, but considers the folly of human beings in general in praying for mistaken goods. And Palamon in turn asks what purpose there is in the way the gods order human life. In all three poems, the situation is remarkably similar: the separation of lovers, a pagan setting, and a philosophical questioning of divine providence in medieval Christian terms. Still more striking, in all three cases, the philosophical questioning derives from Boethius's *De Consolatione Philo-*

sophiae. In the *Troilus*, this origin is perhaps too obvious, and the discussion seems too obviously an afterthought (it occurs only in some manuscripts of the poem). In *The Franklin's Tale* and *The Knight's Tale*, on the other hand, the philosophical questioning flows more naturally from the individual situation, and the argument is passionate, rebellious, and memorable. Arcite asks desperately why men should question the 'purveiaunce of God, or of Fortune' (394), when many, like himself, have desired for themselves apparent goods which have proved disasters. He sums up the situation with a superbly resonant and emphatic line: 'Infinite harmes been in this mateere' (401). He goes on to assert that men seek for the good, but mistake its true nature:

> We faren as he that dronke is as a mous.
> A dronke man woot wel he hath an hous,
> But he noot which the righte wey is thider,
> And to a dronke man the wey is slider.
> And certes, in this world so faren we;
> We seken faste after felicitee,
> But we goon wrong ful often, trewely. (403–9)

The image of the drunkard, more familiar and immediate than we should expect in philosophical discourse, sounds typically Chaucerian, but in fact it, like the argument, is borrowed from Boethius: ' . . . the corage alwey reherseth and seketh the soverein good, al be it so that it be with a derked memorie; but he not by whiche path, right as a dronken man not by whiche path he may retorne him to his hous'.

✳ Palamon

Palamon's speech, which immediately follows, is clearly
intended to parallel Arcite's. Arcite had asked why men
question divine providence; Palamon does question
divine providence, and passionately arraigns the 'crueel
goddes' who govern the world. We have already considered the beast imagery of this speech, and it owes much
of its power to the persistent seriousness with which it
returns to the comparison of man's lot with that of the
animals. The wretchedness of the human lot, as Palamon
conceives it, is made all the more striking by his offering
as the other term of the comparison not the abstract
'animal' but the sheep imagined cowering in its pen:

> What is mankinde moore unto you holde
> Than is the sheep that rouketh in the folde? (449–50)

The thought is again Boethian, but it is transferred to a
pagan setting, and this permits the arraignment of the
divine ordering of the universe to become sharper.
Palamon can bluntly refer to the 'crueel goddes that
governe / This world', while a medieval poet would
probably not feel able to allow one of his characters to
describe the Christian God in such terms. As the poem
progresses we see that the planetary gods who govern its
world are indeed cruel. Chaucer himself was no doubt a
sincere Christian, but in this speech he has realized with
great force an attitude towards the world which in
Christian terms would be blasphemously rebellious. And
the attitude is offered as a challenge to the orthodox
attitude, for the pagan Palamon is made to say:

> The answere of this lete I to divinis,
> But wel I woot that in this world greet pyne is. (464–5)

The force of the speech's pessimism is disturbing, and it is perhaps all the more so in retrospect because the world of the poem turns out to be indeed such as Palamon suggests.

Theseus

This speech of Palamon's occurs at the end of the poem's first part. At the end of the last part, when the main action has come to an end, and Arcite's death has perhaps seemed to suggest that Palamon is right in his arraignment, there occurs another and even more elaborate philosophical speech by Theseus which seems at first sight designed as an answer to Palamon's. It too is Boethian in argument and often in phrasing, and its purpose appears to be to defend divine providence against Palamon's attack. It begins by referring to the 'Firste Moevere of the cause above' (2129), the source of all motion in the universe, identified by medieval scholastic philosophy with the Christian God. It goes on to argue that the mortality and mutability to which the created world is subject are themselves the orderly expression of that unmoved First Mover. Arcite's death, therefore, however unjust it may seem, is in fact part of the divinely established order, and so the witnesses ought not to complain about it. Now it is tempting to see this speech of Theseus as fitting all the events of the poem into an orderly philosophical pattern, so that what had appeared to be the operation of blind Fortune is now disclosed as the working of Providence. But this is not in fact how the speech works as poetry. The grand gesture by which Theseus begins with the origin and end of all philosophizing, the First Mover and First Cause, to justify all particular events is winning, but

its impetus is soon dissipated in repetitions which come
to sound nervously assertive. Thus we find: 'The Firste
Moevere of the cause above...the faire cheyne of love...
that faire cheyne of love....That same Prince and that
Moevere...thilke Moevere....' The more Theseus repeats
himself, the less convincing he sounds. Nor is his case
helped by his assertions that what he is saying is so
obviously true as to be scarcely worth arguing:

> Ther nedeth noght noon auctoritee t'allegge,
> For it is preeved by experience....
> Thanne may men by this ordre wel discerne....
> Wel may men knowe, but it be a fool....
> This maystow understonde and seen at ye....
>
> (2142–3, 2145, 2147, 2158)

What this part of the speech (the first thirty lines, which
come entirely from Boethius, not Boccaccio) seems to
express is above all the *difficulty* philosophy has in ordering the universe. It conveys a sense of strain, a wrenching
and grinding of gears, as Theseus struggles to find order
underlying disorder.

After this come a number of *exempla* of mutability: the
long-lived oak, the hard stone, the broad river, the large
cities, all these come to an end in time, and so must men,
by whatever means. These are more convincing, but what
they prove is not that Arcite's death is just or rational, but,
less ambitiously, that it is what happens to everyone. This
indeed was the gist of the comfort offered by Theseus's
father, Egeus, at the time when Arcite died (1985–91), in
the form not of Boethian philosophy but of folk-wisdom.
Theseus does revert to his First Cause at this point:

> Thanne may I seyn that al this thing moot deye.
> What maketh this but Juppiter, the king,
> That is prince and cause of alle thing,

76

Convertinge al unto his propre welle
From which it is dirrived, sooth to telle? (2176–80)

But the naming of the First Cause as Jupiter immediately
arouses suspicion, for we (unlike Theseus) have been
allowed to see the heavenly pattern behind the poem's
earthly events, and it was one in which Jupiter was power-
less to settle a dispute between Venus and Mars, and
Saturn imposed his will instead. Theseus thinks that the
world of the poem is ruled by the benevolent Jupiter; we
know that it is ruled by the malevolent Saturn. (It would
be possible to argue that by Jupiter here, and in line 2211,
we are to understand simply 'God', and that Theseus,
though a pagan, is to be seen as asserting a Christian view
of the universe. But it is difficult to believe that Chaucer
would admit such an inconsistency into the poem's mythology without warning, and easier to believe that he intends
there to be a gap between Theseus's philosophizing and
the facts of the poem.) He showed a similar obliviousness
in erecting the amphitheatre, a symbol of order crowned by
emblems of disorder. It is difficult not to feel that Theseus,
in his last speech, shares something of the Knight's own
ingenuous attitude towards his story.

At this point a further shift of direction occurs in the
speech:

And heer-agains no creature on live,
Of no degree, availleth for to strive.
Thanne is it wisdom, as it thinketh me,
To maken vertu of necessitee,
And take it weel that we may nat eschue. (2181–5)

From an assertion of order, Theseus has passed to one
of inevitability; and now he leaves metaphysics behind
entirely, and goes on to offer practical advice about the
best way of behaving in a world where change and death

are unavoidable. We must make a virtue of necessity: rejoice that Arcite's death occurred when his glory was at its height, and that now at last he has escaped from 'this foule prisoun of this lyf'. And finally, with a certain self-consciousness about the length and complication of his argument, Theseus adds:

> What may I conclude of this longe serye,
> But after wo I rede us to be merye,
> And thanken Juppiter of al his grace? (2209–11)

The reference to Jupiter again rings hollow; what 'grace' of his has been displayed in the story we have been following? But Theseus concludes his speech with more definite and practical advice: let Emelye accept Palamon as her husband, and turn the sorrow of funeral into the joy of marriage. Emelye and Palamon silently acquiesce in this arrangement, and the poem ends with their wedding and 'happy ever after'. Thus the pessimism which has so far reigned is mitigated at the last moment, not by being refuted, but by being allowed to fade from our attention. Theseus has moved from unconvincing philosophical speculation to sensible practical advice; he has not shown that all is for the best in the world of the poem, but he has shown how to go on living in a world ruled by Saturn.[1]

---

[1] A recent book on Chaucer has described this as a 'damning comment' on Theseus's speech, but it was not intended as such. To show 'how to go on living in a world ruled by Saturn' is an achievement of the highest importance, and perhaps one fundamental to civilisation itself.

CONCLUSION

The final effect, then, of *The Knight's Tale* is neither optimistic nor tragic. It is pessimistic and yet sensible, with a good sense that we may think of as typically Chaucerian. The poem has included some comedy of a rather cruel kind, in its view of human beings—Theseus as well as the two lovers—as deluded instruments of powers who care little for them. The twentieth century can perhaps legitimately see in this fourteenth-century poem a view of the human condition as neither comic nor tragic but absurd—a view of life similar to that expressed by a modern writer such as Samuel Beckett and found in Shakespeare by a modern critic such as Jan Kott. The poem's view of life does not seem to me to be that of orthodox medieval Christianity, nor is it necessarily Chaucer's own total and final view. For that we must no doubt turn to the 'Retracciouns' at the end of *The Canterbury Tales*, in which he renounces all his 'enditinges of worldly vanitees'. But it does express an attitude which a medieval Christian, like a man of any other period, might feel forced upon him from time to time, at least as a possibility. Perhaps the world is ruled by Saturn: this is the hypothesis into which *The Knight's Tale* invites us to enter, and it is all the more challenging and disturbing a poem because its view of human life is not pure but dubious and mixed.

NOTE ON THE TEXT

The text which follows is based upon that of F. N. Robinson (*The Complete Works of Geoffrey Chaucer*, 2nd ed., 1957). The punctuation has been revised, with special reference to the exclamation marks. Spelling has been partly rationalized, by substituting *i* for *y* wherever the change aids the modern reader and does not affect the semantic value of the word. Thus *smylyng* becomes 'smiling', and *nyghtyngale* 'nightingale', but *wyn* (wine), *lyk* (like), and *fyr* (fire) are allowed to stand.

No accentuation has been provided in this text, for two reasons. First, because it produces a page displeasing to the eye; secondly, because it no longer seems necessary or entirely reliable in the light of modern scholarship. It is not now thought that the later works of Chaucer were written in a ten-syllable line from which no variation was permissible. The correct reading of a line of Chaucer is now seen to be more closely related to the correct reading of a comparable line of prose with phrasing suited to the rhythms of speech. This allows the reader to be more flexible in his interpretation of the line, and makes it unreasonably pedantic to provide a rigid system of accentuation.

NOTE ON PRONUNCIATION

These equivalences are intended to offer only a rough guide. For further detail, see *An Introduction to Chaucer*.

SHORT VOWELS

ă represents the sound now written *u*, as in 'cut'
ĕ as in modern 'set'
ĭ as in modern 'is'
ŏ as in modern 'top'
ŭ as in modern 'put' (not as in 'cut')
final -*e* represents the neutral vowel sound in '*a*bout' or 'attent*io*n'. It is silent when the next word in the line begins with a vowel or an *h*.

Note on the Text

ā as in modern 'car' (not as in 'name')

ē (open—i.e. where the equivalent modern word is spelt with *ea*) as in modern 'there'

ē (close—i.e. where the equivalent modern word is spelt with *ee* or *e*) represents the sound now written *a* as in 'take'

ī as in modern 'machine' (not as in 'like')

ō (open—i.e. where the equivalent modern vowel is pronounced as in 'br*o*ther', 'm*ood*', or '*good*') represents the sound now written *aw* as in 'fawn'

ō (close—i.e. where the equivalent modern vowel is pronounced as in 'road') as in modern 'note'

ū as in French *tu* or German *Tür*.

DIPHTHONGS

ai and *ei* both roughly represent the sound now written *i* or *y* as in 'die' or 'dye'

au and *aw* both represent the sound now written *ow* or *ou* as in 'now' or 'pounce'

ou and *ow* have two pronunciations: as in *through* where the equivalent modern vowel is pronounced as in 'through' or 'mouse'; and as in *pounce* where the equivalent modern vowel is pronounced as in 'know' or 'thought'.

WRITING OF VOWELS AND DIPHTHONGS

A long vowel is often indicated by doubling, as in *roote* or *eek*. The *ŭ* sound is sometimes represented by an *o* as in *yong*. The *au* sound is sometimes represented by an *a*, especially before *m* or *n*, as in *cha(u)mbre* or *cha(u)nce*.

CONSONANTS

Largely as in modern English, except that many consonants now silent were still pronounced. *Gh* was pronounced as in Scottish 'lo*ch*', and both consonants should be pronounced in such groups as the following: '*gn*acchen', '*kn*ave', 'wo*rd*', 'fo*lk*', '*wr*ong'.

THE KNIGHT'S TALE

PART I

Whilom, as olde stories tellen us,
Ther was a duc that highte Theseus;
Of Atthenes he was lord and governour,
And in his time swich a conquerour
That gretter was ther noon under the sonne.
Ful many a riche contree hadde he wonne;
What with his wisdom and his chivalrie,
He conquered al the regne of Femenye,
That whilom was ycleped Scithia,
And weddede the queene Ypolita,   10
And broghte hire hoom with him in his contree
With muchel glorie and greet solempnitee,
And eek hir yonge suster Emelye.
And thus with victorie and with melodye
Lete I this noble duc to Atthenes ride,
And al his hoost in armes him biside.

And certes, if it nere to long to heere,
I wolde have toold yow fully the manere
How wonnen was the regne of Femenye
By Theseus and by his chivalrye;   20
And of the grete bataille for the nones
Bitwixen Atthenes and Amazones;
And how asseged was Ypolita,
The faire, hardy queene of Scithia;
And of the feste that was at hir weddinge,
And of the tempest at hir hoom-cominge;
But al that thing I moot as now forbere.
I have, God woot, a large feeld to ere,

And wayke been the oxen in my plough.
30 The remenant of the tale is long ynough.
I wol nat letten eek noon of this route;
Lat every felawe telle his tale aboute,
And lat se now who shal the soper winne;
And ther I lefte, I wol ayeyn biginne.

This duc of whom I make mencioun,
Whan he was come almoost unto the toun,
In al his wele and in his mooste pride,
He was war, as he caste his eye aside,
Where that ther kneled in the heighe weye
40 A compaignye of ladies, tweye and tweye,
Ech after oother, clad in clothes blake;
But swich a cry and swich a wo they make
That in this world nis creature livinge
That herde swich another waymentinge;
And of this cry they nolde nevere stenten
Til they the reines of his bridel henten.

'What folk been ye, that at myn hom-cominge
Perturben so my feste with cryinge?'
Quod Theseus. 'Have ye so greet envye
50 Of myn honour, that thus compleyne and crye?
Or who hath yow misboden or offended?
And telleth me if it may been amended,
And why that ye been clothed thus in blak.'

The eldeste lady of hem alle spak,
Whan she hadde swowned with a deedly cheere,
That it was routhe for to seen and heere.
She seyde: 'Lord, to whom Fortune hath yiven
Victorie, and as a conqueror to liven,
Nat greveth us youre glorie and youre honour,
60 But we biseken mercy and socour.

84

Have mercy on oure wo and oure distresse.
Som drope of pitee, thurgh thy gentillesse,
Upon us wrecched wommen lat thou falle.
For certes, lord, ther is noon of us alle
That she ne hath been a duchesse or a queene.
Now be we caytyves, as it is wel seene,
Thanked be Fortune and hire false wheel,
That noon estaat assureth to be weel.
And certes, lord, to abiden youre presence,
Heere in this temple of the goddesse Clemence   70
We han ben waitinge al this fourtenight.
Now help us, lord, sith it is in thy might.

    I, wrecche, which that wepe and waile thus,
Was whilom wyf to king Cappaneus,
That starf at Thebes—cursed be that day!—
And alle we that been in this array
And maken al this lamentacioun,
We losten alle oure housbondes at that toun
Whil that the seege theraboute lay.
And yet now the olde Creon, weylaway!   80
That lord is now of Thebes the citee,
Fulfild of ire and of iniquitee,
He, for despit and for his tirannye,
To do the dede bodies vileynye
Of alle oure lordes whiche that been yslawe,
Hath alle the bodies on an heep ydrawe,
And wol nat suffren hem, by noon assent,
Neither to been yburied nor ybrent,
But maketh houndes ete hem in despit.'

    And with that word, withouten moore respit,   90
They fillen gruf and criden pitously,
'Have on us wrecched wommen som mercy,

85

And lat oure sorwe sinken in thyn herte.'

This gentil duc doun from his courser sterte
With herte pitous, whan he herde hem speke.
Him thoughte that his herte wolde breke,
Whan he saugh hem so pitous and so maat,
That whilom weren of so greet estaat;
And in his armes he hem alle up hente,
And hem conforteth in ful good entente,
And swoor his ooth, as he was trewe knight,
He wolde doon so ferforthly his might
Upon the tiraunt Creon hem to wreke,
That al the peple of Grece sholde speke
How Creon was of Theseus yserved
As he that hadde his deeth ful wel deserved.
And right anoon, withouten moore abood,
His baner he desplayeth, and forth rood
To Thebes-ward, and al his hoost biside.
No neer Atthenes wolde he go ne ride,
Ne take his ese fully half a day,
But onward on his wey that night he lay,
And sente anon Ypolita the queene
And Emelye, hir yonge suster sheene,
Unto the toun of Atthenes to dwelle,
And forth he rit; ther is namoore to telle.

The rede statue of Mars, with spere and targe,
So shineth in his white baner large
That alle the feeldes gliteren up and doun;
And by his baner born is his penoun
Of gold ful riche, in which ther was ybete
The Minotaur, which that he slough in Crete.
Thus rit this duc, thus rit this conquerour,
And in his hoost of chivalrie the flour,

Til that he cam to Thebes and alighte
Faire in a feeld, ther as he thoughte to fighte.
But shortly for to speken of this thing,
With Creon, which that was of Thebes king,
He faught, and slough him manly as a knight
In pleyn bataille, and putte the folk to flight; 130
And by assaut he wan the citee after,
And rente adoun bothe wall and sparre and rafter;
And to the ladies he restored again
The bones of hir housbondes that were slain,
To doon obsequies, as was tho the gyse.
But it were al to longe for to devyse
The grete clamour and the waymentinge
That the ladies made at the brenninge
Of the bodies, and the grete honour
That Theseus, the noble conquerour, 140
Dooth to the ladies whan they from him wente;
But shortly for to telle is myn entente.

 Whan that this worthy duc, this Theseus,
Hath Creon slain, and wonne Thebes thus,
Stille in that feeld he took al night his reste,
And dide with al the contree as him leste.

 To ransake in the taas of bodies dede,
Hem for to strepe of harneys and of wede,
The pilours diden bisynesse and cure
After the bataille and disconfiture. 150
And so bifel that in the taas they founde,
Thurgh-girt with many a grevous blody wounde,
Two yonge knightes ligginge by and by,
Bothe in oon armes, wroght ful richely,
Of whiche two Arcita highte that oon,
And that oother knight highte Palamon.

Nat fully quyke, ne fully dede they were,
But by hir cote-armures and by hir gere
The heraudes knewe hem best in special
160 As they that weren of the blood roial
Of Thebes, and of sustren two yborn.
Out of the taas the pilours han hem torn,
And han hem caried softe unto the tente
Of Theseus; and he ful soone hem sente
To Atthenes, to dwellen in prisoun
Perpetuelly—he nolde no raunsoun.
And whan this worthy duc hath thus ydon,
He took his hoost, and hoom he rit anon
With laurer crowned as a conquerour;
170 And ther he liveth in joye and in honour
Terme of his lyf; what nedeth wordes mo?
And in a tour, in angwissh and in wo,
This Palamon and his felawe Arcite
For everemoore; ther may no gold hem quite.

This passeth yeer by yeer and day by day,
Till it fil ones, in a morwe of May,
That Emelye, that fairer was to sene
Than is the lilie upon his stalke grene,
And fressher than the May with floures newe—
180 For with the rose colour stroof hire hewe,
I noot which was the finer of hem two—
Er it were day, as was hir wone to do,
She was arisen and al redy dight;
For May wole have no slogardie a-night.
The sesoun priketh every gentil herte,
And maketh him out of his slep to sterte,
And seith 'Arys and do thyn observaunce.'
This maked Emelye have remembraunce

To doon honour to May, and for to rise.
Yclothed was she fressh, for to devyse: 190
Hir yelow heer was broided in a tresse
Bihinde hir bak, a yerde long, I gesse.
And in the gardyn, at the sonne upriste,
She walketh up and doun, and as hire liste
She gadereth floures, party white and rede,
To make a subtil gerland for hire hede;
And as an aungel hevenisshly she soong.
The grete tour, that was so thikke and stroong,
Which of the castel was the chief dongeoun
(Ther as the knightes weren in prisoun   200
Of which I tolde yow and tellen shal)
Was evene joinant to the gardyn wal
Ther as this Emelye hadde hir pleyinge.
Bright was the sonne and cleer that morweninge,
And Palamoun, this woful prisoner,
As was his wone, by leve of his gayler
Was risen and romed in a chambre an heigh,
In which he al the noble citee seigh,
And eek the gardyn, ful of braunches grene,
Ther as this fresshe Emelye the shene   210
Was in hire walk, and romed up and doun.
This sorweful prisoner, this Palamoun,
Goth in the chambre rominge to and fro,
And to himself compleyninge of his wo.
That he was born, ful ofte he seyde, 'allas!'
And so bifel, by aventure or cas,
That thurgh a window, thikke of many a barre
Of iren greet and square as any sparre,
He cast his eye upon Emelya,
And therwithal he bleynte and cride, 'A!'   220

As though he stongen were unto the herte.
And with that cry Arcite anon up sterte,
And seyde, 'Cosin myn, what eyleth thee,
That art so pale and deedly on to see?
Why cridestow? Who hath thee doon offence?
For Goddes love, taak al in pacience
Oure prisoun, for it may noon oother be.
Fortune hath yeven us this adversitee.
Som wikke aspect or disposicioun
230   Of Saturne, by som constellacioun,
Hath yeven us this, although we hadde it sworn;
So stood the hevene whan that we were born.
We moste endure it; this is the short and plain.'
     This Palamon answerde and seyde again:
'Cosin, for sothe, of this opinioun
Thow hast a veyn imaginacioun.
This prison caused me nat for to crye,
But I was hurt right now thurghout myn ye
Into myn herte, that wol my bane be.
240   The fairnesse of that lady that I see
Yond in the gardyn romen to and fro
Is cause of al my crying and my wo.
I noot wher she be womman or goddesse,
But Venus is it soothly, as I gesse.'
And therwithal on knees doun he fil,
And seyde: 'Venus, if it be thy wil
Yow in this gardyn thus to transfigure
Bifore me, sorweful, wrecched creature,
Out of this prisoun help that we may scapen.
250   And if so be my destinee be shapen
By eterne word to dyen in prisoun,
Of oure linage have som compassioun,

That is so lowe ybroght by tirannye.'
And with that word Arcite gan espye
Wher as this lady romed to and fro,
And with that sighte hir beautee hurte him so,
That, if that Palamon was wounded sore,
Arcite is hurt as muche as he, or moore.
And with a sigh he seyde pitously:
'The fresshe beautee sleeth me sodeynly   260
Of hire that rometh in the yonder place,
And but I have hir mercy and hir grace,
That I may seen hire atte leeste weye,
I nam but deed; ther nis namoore to seye.'

   This Palamon, whan he tho wordes herde,
Dispitously he looked and answerde,
'Wheither seistow this in ernest or in pley?'

   'Nay,' quod Arcite, 'in ernest, by my fey?
God helpe me so, me list ful yvele pleye.'

   This Palamon gan knitte his browes tweye.   270
'It nere,' quod he, 'to thee no greet honour
For to be fals ne for to be traitour
To me, that am thy cosin and thy brother
Ysworn ful depe, and ech of us til oother,
That nevere, for to dyen in the peyne,
Til that the deeth departe shal us tweyne,
Neither of us in love to hindre oother,
Ne in noon oother cas, my leeve brother;
But that thou sholdest trewely forthren me
In every cas, as I shal forthren thee—   280
This was thyn ooth, and myn also, certeyn;
I woot right wel, thou darst it nat withseyn.
Thus artow of my conseil, out of doute,
And now thow woldest falsly been aboute

To love my lady, whom I love and serve,
And evere shal til that myn herte sterve.
Nay, certes, false Arcite, thow shalt nat so.
I loved hire first, and tolde thee my wo
As to my conseil and my brother sworn
To forthre me, as I have toold biforn.
For which thou art ybounden as a knight
To helpen me, if it lay in thy might,
Or elles artow fals, I dar wel seyn.'

   This Arcite ful proudly spak ageyn:
'Thow shalt,' quod he, 'be rather fals than I;
And thou art fals, I telle thee outrely,
For paramour I loved hire first er thow.
What wiltow seyen? Thou woost nat yet now
Wheither she be a womman or goddesse!
Thyn is affeccioun of hoolinesse,
And myn is love, as to a creature;
For which I tolde thee myn aventure
As to my cosin and my brother sworn.
I pose that thow lovedest hire biforn;
Wostow nat wel the olde clerkes sawe,
That "who shal yeve a lovere any lawe?"
Love is a gretter lawe, by my pan,
Than may be yeve to any erthely man;
And therfore positif lawe and swich decree
Is broken al day for love in ech degree.
A man moot nedes love, maugree his heed.
He may nat fleen it thogh he sholde be deed,
Al be she maide, or widwe, or elles wyf.
And eek it is nat likly al thy lyf
To stonden in hir grace; namoore shal I;
For wel thou woost thyselven, verraily,

That thou and I be dampned to prisoun
Perpetuelly; us gaineth no raunsoun.
We strive as dide the houndes for the boon;
They foughte al day, and yet hir part was noon.   320
Ther cam a kite, whil that they were so wrothe,
And baar awey the boon bitwixe hem bothe.
And therfore, at the kinges court, my brother,
Ech man for himself, ther is noon oother.
Love, if thee list, for I love and ay shal;
And soothly, leeve brother, this is al.
Heere in this prisoun moote we endure,
And everich of us take his aventure.'

   Greet was the strif and long bitwix hem tweye,
If that I hadde leyser for to seye,   330
But to th'effect. It happed on a day,
To telle it yow as shortly as I may,
A worthy duc that highte Perotheus,
That felawe was unto duc Theseus
Sin thilke day that they were children lite,
Was come to Atthenes his felawe to visite,
And for to pleye as he was wont to do;
For in this world he loved no man so,
And he loved him als tendrely again.
So wel they lovede, as olde bookes sayn,   340
That whan that oon was deed, soothly to telle,
His felawe wente and soughte him doun in helle;
But of that storie list me nat to write.
Duc Perotheus loved wel Arcite,
And hadde him knowe at Thebes yeer by yere,
And finally at requeste and preyere
Of Perotheus, withouten any raunsoun,
Duc Theseus him leet out of prisoun

Frely to goon wher that him liste over al,
350 In swich a gyse as I you tellen shal.

This was the forward, pleynly for t'endite,
Bitwixen Theseus and him Arcite
That if so were that Arcite were yfounde
Evere in his lif, by day or night, oo stounde
In any contree of this Theseus,
And he were caught, it was acorded thus,
That with a swerd he sholde lese his heed.
Ther nas noon oother remedie ne reed;
But taketh his leve, and homward he him spedde.
360 Lat him be war! his nekke lith to wedde.

How greet a sorwe suffreth now Arcite!
The deeth he feeleth thurgh his herte smite;
He wepeth, waileth, crieth pitously;
To sleen himself he waiteth prively.
He seyde, 'Allas that day that I was born!
Now is my prisoun worse than biforn;
Now is me shape eternally to dwelle
Noght in purgatorie, but in helle.
Allas, that evere knew I Perotheus!
370 For elles hadde I dwelled with Theseus,
Yfetered in his prisoun everemo.
Thanne hadde I been in blisse and nat in wo.
Oonly the sighte of hire whom that I serve,
Though that I nevere hir grace may deserve,
Wolde han suffised right ynough for me.
O deere cosin Palamon,' quod he,
'Thyn is the victorie of this aventure.
Ful blisfully in prison maistow dure—
In prison? certes nay, but in paradys.
380 Wel hath Fortune yturned thee the dys,

That hast the sighte of hire, and I th'absence.
For possible is, sin thou hast hire presence,
And art a knight, a worthy and an able,
That by som cas, sin Fortune is chaungeable,
Thow maist to thy desir somtime atteyne.
But I, that am exiled and bareyne
Of alle grace, and in so greet dispeir,
That ther nis erthe, water, fir, ne eir,
Ne creature that of hem maked is,
That may me helpe or doon confort in this,   390
Wel oughte I sterve in wanhope and distresse.
Farwel my lif, my lust, and my gladnesse!

   Allas, why pleynen folk so in commune
On purveiaunce of God, or of Fortune,
That yeveth hem ful ofte in many a gyse
Wel bettre than they kan hemself devyse?
Som man desireth for to han richesse,
That cause is of his mordre or greet siknesse;
And som man wolde out of his prisoun fain,
That in his hous is of his meynee slain.   400
Infinite harmes been in this mateere.
We witen nat what thing we preyen heere:
We faren as he that dronke is as a mous.
A dronke man woot wel he hath an hous,
But he noot which the righte wey is thider,
And to a dronke man the wey is slider.
And certes, in this world so faren we;
We seken faste after felicitee,
But we goon wrong ful often, trewely.
Thus may we seyen alle, and namely I,   410
That wende and hadde a greet opinioun
That if I mighte escapen from prisoun

Thanne hadde I been in joye and perfit heele,
Ther now I am exiled fro my wele.
Sin that I may nat seen you, Emelye,
I nam but deed; ther nis no remedye.'

    Upon that oother side Palamon,
Whan that he wiste Arcite was agon,
Swich sorwe he maketh that the grete tour
420   Resouneth of his youling and clamour.
The pure fettres on his shynes grete
Weren of his bittre, salte teeres wete.
'Allas,' quod he, 'Arcita, cosin myn,
Of al oure strif, God woot, the fruit is thyn.
Thow walkest now in Thebes at thy large,
And of my wo thow yevest litel charge.
Thou mayst, sin thou hast wisdom and manhede,
Assemblen alle the folk of oure kinrede,
And make a werre so sharp on this citee,
430   That by som aventure or some tretee
Thow mayst have hire to lady and to wyf
For whom that I moste nedes lese my lyf.
For, as by wey of possibilitee,
Sith thou art at thy large, of prisoun free,
And art a lord, greet is thyn avauntage
Moore than is myn, that sterve here in a cage.
For I moot wepe and waile, whil I live,
With al the wo that prison may me yive,
And eek with peyne that love me yeveth also,
440   That doubleth al my torment and my wo.'
Therwith the fyr of jalousie up sterte
Withinne his brest, and hente him by the herte
So woodly that he lyk was to biholde
The boxtree or the asshen dede and colde.

Thanne seyde he, 'O crueel goddes that governe
This world with binding of youre word eterne,
And writen in the table of atthamaunt
Youre parlement and youre eterne graunt,
What is mankinde moore unto you holde
Than is the sheep that rouketh in the folde?   450
For slain is man right as another beest,
And dwelleth eek in prison and arreest,
And hath siknesse and greet adversitee,
And ofte times giltelees, pardee.

What governance is in this prescience,
That giltelees tormenteth innocence?
And yet encresseth this al my penaunce,
That man is bounden to his observaunce,
For Goddes sake, to letten of his wille,
Ther as a beest may al his lust fulfille.   460
And whan a beest is deed he hath no peyne;
But man after his deeth moot wepe and pleyne,
Though in this world he have care and wo.
Withouten doute it may stonden so.
The answere of this lete I to divinis,
But wel I woot that in this world greet pyne is.
Allas, I se a serpent or a theef,
That many a trewe man hath doon mescheef,
Goon at his large, and where him list may turne.
But I moot been in prisoun thurgh Saturne,   470
And eek thurgh Juno, jalous and eek wood,
That hath destroyed wel ny al the blood
Of Thebes with his waste walles wide;
And Venus sleeth me on that oother side
For jalousie and fere of him Arcite.'

Now wol I stynte of Palamon a lite,

97

And lete him in his prisoun stille dwelle,
And of Arcita forth I wol yow telle.

The somer passeth, and the nightes longe
480 Encressen double wise the peynes stronge
Bothe of the lovere and the prisoner.
I noot which hath the wofuller mester.
For, shortly for to seyn, this Palamoun
Perpetuelly is dampned to prisoun,
In cheynes and in fettres to been deed;
And Arcite is exiled upon his heed
For everemo, as out of that contree,
Ne nevere mo he shal his lady see.

Yow loveres axe I now this questioun:
490 Who hath the worse, Arcite or Palamoun?
That oon may seen his lady day by day,
But in prison he moot dwelle alway;
That oother wher him list may ride or go,
But seen his lady shal he nevere mo.
Now demeth as yow liste, ye that kan,
For I wol telle forth as I bigan.

PART II

Whan that Arcite to Thebes comen was,
Ful ofte a day he swelte and seyde 'Allas!'
For seen his lady shal he nevere mo.
500 And shortly to concluden al his wo,
So muche sorwe hadde nevere creature
That is, or shal, whil that the world may dure.
His slep, his mete, his drinke, is him biraft,
That lene he wex and drye as is a shaft;
His eyen holwe, and grisly to biholde,

His hewe falow and pale as asshen colde,
And solitarie he was and evere allone,
And waillinge al the night, makinge his mone;
And if he herde song or instrument,
Thanne wolde he wepe, he mighte nat be stent.   510
So feble eek were his spiritz, and so lowe,
And chaunged so, that no man koude knowe
His speche nor his vois, though men it herde.
And in his geere for al the world he ferde,
Nat oonly lik the loveris maladye
Of Hereos, but rather lyk manie,
Engendred of humour malencolik,
Biforen, in his celle fantastik.
And shortly, turned was al up so doun
Bothe habit and eek disposicioun   520
Of him, this woful lovere daun Arcite.

    What sholde I al day of his wo endite?
Whan he endured hadde a yeer or two
This crueel torment and this peyne and wo,
At Thebes, in his contree, as I seyde,
Upon a night in sleep as he him leyde
Him thoughte how that the winged god Mercurie
Biforn him stood and bad him to be murie.
His slepy yerde in hond he bar uprighte;
An hat he werede upon his heris brighte.   530
Arrayed was this god, as he took keep,
As he was whan that Argus took his sleep;
And seyde him thus: 'To Atthenes shaltou wende,
Ther is thee shapen of thy wo an ende.'
And with that word Arcite wook and sterte.
'Now trewely, hou soore that me smerte,'
Quod he, 'to Atthenes right now wol I fare,

Ne for the drede of deeth shal I nat spare
To se my lady that I love and serve.
540   In hire presence I recche nat to sterve.'
    And with that word he caughte a greet mirour
And saugh that chaunged was al his colour,
And saugh his visage al in another kinde.
And right anon it ran him in his minde,
That, sith his face was so disfigured
Of maladye the which he hadde endured,
He mighte wel, if that he bar him lowe,
Live in Atthenes everemoore unknowe,
And seen his lady wel ny day by day.
550   And right anon he chaunged his array,
And cladde him as a povre laborer,
And al allone, save oonly a squier
That knew his privetee and al his cas,
Which was disgised povrely as he was,
To Atthenes is he goon the nexte way.
And to the court he wente upon a day,
And at the gate he profreth his servise
To drugge and drawe, what so men wol devyse,
And shortly of this matere for to seyn,
560   He fil in office with a chamberleyn
The which that dwellinge was with Emelye;
For he was wys and koude soone espye
Of every servaunt which that serveth here.
Wel koude he hewen wode, and water bere,
For he was yong and mighty for the nones,
And therto he was long and big of bones
To doon that any wight kan him devyse.
A yeer or two he was in this servise,
Page of the chambre of Emelye the brighte;

And Philostrate he seyde that he highte. 570
But half so wel biloved a man as he
Ne was ther nevere in court of his degree;
He was so gentil of condicioun
That thurghout al the court was his renoun.
They seyden that it were a charitee
That Theseus wolde enhauncen his degree,
And putten him in worshipful servise,
Ther as he mighte his vertu excercise.
And thus withinne a while his name is spronge,
Bothe of his dedes and his goode tonge, 580
That Theseus hath taken him so neer
That of his chambre he made him a squier,
And gaf him gold to maintene his degree.
And eek men broghte him out of his contree,
From yeer to yeer, ful prively his rente;
But honestly and slyly he it spente,
That no man wondred how that he it hadde.
And thre yeer in this wise his lif he ladde,
And bar him so, in pees and eek in werre,
Ther was no man that Theseus hath derre. 590
And in this blisse lete I now Arcite,
And speke I wole of Palamon a lite.

   In derknesse and horrible and strong prisoun
Thise seven yeer hath seten Palamoun
Forpined, what for wo and for distresse.
Who feeleth double soor and hevinesse
But Palamon, that love destreyneth so
That wood out of his wit he goth for wo?
And eek therto he is a prisoner
Perpetuelly, noght oonly for a yer. 600
   Who koude rime in Englissh proprely

His martirdom? for sothe it am nat I;
Therfore I passe as lightly as I may.
    It fel that in the seventhe yer, of May
The thridde night, (as olde bookes seyn,
That al this storie tellen moore pleyn)
Were it by aventure or destinee—
As, whan a thing is shapen, it shal be—
That soone after the midnight Palamoun,
By helping of a freend, brak his prisoun
And fleeth the citee faste as he may go.
For he hadde yeve his gayler drinke so
Of a clarree maad of a certeyn wyn,
With nercotikes and opie of Thebes fyn,
That al that night, thogh that men wolde him shake,
The gayler sleep, he mighte nat awake;
And thus he fleeth as faste as evere he may.
The night was short and faste by the day,
That nedes cost he moot himselven hide;
And til a grove faste ther biside
With dredeful foot thanne stalketh Palamon.
For, shortly, this was his opinion,
That in that grove he wolde him hide al day,
And in the night thanne wolde he take his way
To Thebes-ward, his freendes for to preye
On Theseus to helpe him to werreye;
And shortly, outher he wolde lese his lif,
Or winnen Emelye unto his wyf.
This is th'effect and his entente pleyn.
    Now wol I turne to Arcite ageyn,
That litel wiste how ny that was his care,
Til that Fortune had broght him in the snare.
    The bisy larke, messager of day,

610

620

630

Salueth in hir song the morwe gray,
And firy Phebus riseth up so bright
That al the orient laugheth of the light,
And with his stremes dryeth in the greves
The silver dropes hanginge on the leves.
And Arcita, that in the court roial
With Theseus is squier principal,   640
Is risen and looketh on the myrie day.
And for to doon his observaunce to May,
Remembringe on the point of his desir,
He on a courser, startlinge as the fir,
Is riden into the feeldes him to pleye,
Out of the court, were it a mile or tweye.
And to the grove of which that I yow tolde
By aventure his wey he gan to holde,
To maken him a gerland of the greves
Were it of wodebinde or hawethorn leves,   650
And loude he song ayeyn the sonne shene:
'May, with alle thy floures and thy grene,
Welcome be thou, faire, fresshe May,
In hope that I som grene gete may.'
And from his courser, with a lusty herte,
Into the grove ful hastily he sterte,
And in a path he rometh up and doun,
Ther as by aventure this Palamoun
Was in a bussh, that no man mighte him se,
For soore afered of his deeth was he.   660
No thing ne knew he that it was Arcite;
God woot he wolde have trowed it ful lite.
But sooth is seyd, go sithen many yeres,
That 'feeld hath eyen and the wode hath eres.'
It is ful fair a man to bere him evene,

For al day meeteth men at unset stevene.
Ful litel woot Arcite of his felawe,
That was so ny to herknen al his sawe,
For in the bussh he sitteth now ful stille.

670   Whan that Arcite hadde romed al his fille,
And songen al the roundel lustily,
Into a studie he fil sodeynly,
As doon thise loveres in hir queynte geres,
Now in the crope, now doun in the breres,
Now up, now doun, as boket in a welle.
Right as the Friday, soothly for to telle,
Now it shineth, now it reyneth faste,
Right so kan geery Venus overcaste
The hertes of hir folk; right as hir day
680 Is gereful, right so chaungeth she array.
Selde is the Friday al the wowke ylike.

   Whan that Arcite had songe, he gan to sike,
And sette him doun withouten any moore.
'Allas,' quod he, 'that day that I was bore!
How longe, Juno, thurgh thy crueltee,
Woltow werreyen Thebes the citee?
Allas, ybroght is to confusioun
The blood roial of Cadme and Amphioun—
Of Cadmus, which that was the firste man
690 That Thebes bulte, or first the toun bigan,
And of the citee first was crouned king.
Of his linage am I and his ofspring
By verray ligne, as of the stok roial,
And now I am so caytyf and so thral
That he that is my mortal enemy,
I serve him as his squier povrely.
And yet dooth Juno me wel moore shame,

For I dar noght biknowe myn owene name;
But ther as I was wont to highte Arcite,
Now highte I Philostrate, noght worth a mite.   700
Allas, thou felle Mars, allas, Juno!
Thus hath youre ire oure linage al fordo,
Save oonly me and wrecched Palamoun,
That Theseus martireth in prisoun.
And over al this, to sleen me outrely,
Love hath his firy dart so brenningly
Ystiked thurgh my trewe, careful herte,
That shapen was my deeth erst than my sherte.
Ye sleen me with youre eyen, Emelye;
Ye been the cause wherfore that I die.   710
Of al the remenant of myn oother care
Ne sette I nat the montance of a tare,
So that I koude doon aught to youre plesaunce.'
And with that word he fil doun in a traunce
A longe time, and after he up sterte.
    This Palamoun, that thoughte that thurgh his herte
He felte a coold swerd sodeynliche glide,
For ire he quook, no lenger wolde he bide.
And whan that he had herd Arcites tale,
As he were wood, with face deed and pale,   720
He stirte him up out of the buskes thikke,
And seide: 'Arcite, false traitour wikke,
Now artow hent, that lovest my lady so,
For whom that I have al this peyne and wo,
And art my blood, and to my conseil sworn,
As I ful ofte have told thee heerbiforn,
And hast byjaped heere duc Theseus,
And falsly chaunged hast thy name thus!
I wol be deed, or elles thou shalt die.

730 Thou shalt nat love my lady Emelye,
But I wol love hire oonly and namo;
For I am Palamon, thy mortal foo.
And though that I no wepene have in this place,
But out of prison am astert by grace,
I drede noght that outher thow shalt die,
Or thow ne shalt nat loven Emelye.
Chees which thou wolt, for thou shalt nat asterte.'
    This Arcite, with ful despitous herte,
Whan he him knew, and hadde his tale herd,
740 As fiers as leon pulled out his swerd,
And seyde thus: 'By God that sit above,
Nere it that thou art sik and wood for love,
And eek that thow no wepne hast in this place,
Thou sholdest nevere out of this grove pace
That thou ne sholdest dyen of myn hond.
For I defye the seurete and the bond
Which that thou seist that I have maad to thee.
What, verray fool, think wel that love is free,
And I wol love hire maugree al thy might!
750 But for as muche thou art a worthy knight,
And wilnest to darreyne hire by bataille,
Have heer my trouthe, tomorwe I wol nat faille,
Withoute witing of any oother wight,
That heere I wol be founden as a knight,
And bringen harneys right ynough for thee;
And ches the beste, and leef the worste for me.
And mete and drinke this night wol I bringe
Ynough for thee, and clothes for thy beddinge.
And if so be that thou my lady winne,
760 And sle me in this wode ther I am inne,
Thow mayst wel have thy lady as for me.'

This Palamon answerde, 'I graunte it thee.'
And thus they been departed til amorwe,
Whan ech of hem had leyd his feith to borwe.
   O Cupide, out of alle charitee!
O regne, that wolt no felawe have with thee!
Ful sooth is seyd that love ne lordshipe
Wol noght, his thankes, have no felaweshipe.
Wel finden that Arcite and Palamoun.
Arcite is riden anon unto the toun,   770
And on the morwe, er it were dayes light,
Ful prively two harneys hath he dight,
Bothe suffisaunt and mete to darreyne
The bataille in the feeld bitwix hem tweyne;
And on his hors, allone as he was born,
He carieth al the harneys him biforn.
And in the grove, at time and place yset,
This Arcite and this Palamon ben met.
Tho chaungen gan the colour in hir face,
Right as the hunters in the regne of Trace,   780
That stondeth at the gappe with a spere,
Whan hunted is the leon or the bere,
And hereth him come russhing in the greves,
And breketh bothe bowes and the leves,
And thinketh, 'Heere cometh my mortal enemy!
Withoute faille, he moot be deed, or I;
For outher I moot sleen him at the gappe,
Or he moot sleen me, if that me mishappe,'—
So ferden they in chaunging of hir hewe,
As fer as everich of hem oother knewe.   790
   Ther nas no good day, ne no saluing,
But streight, withouten word or rehersing,
Everich of hem heelp for to armen oother

As freendly as he were his owene brother;
And after that, with sharpe speres stronge
They foynen ech at oother wonder longe.
Thou mightest wene that this Palamon
In his fighting were a wood leon,
And as a crueel tigre was Arcite;
As wilde bores gonne they to smite,
That frothen whit as foom for ire wood.
Up to the ancle foghte they in hir blood.
And in this wise I lete hem fighting dwelle,
And forth I wole of Theseus yow telle.

　　The destinee, ministre general,
That executeth in the world over al
The purveiaunce that God hath seyn biforn,
So strong it is that, though the world had sworn
The contrarie of a thing by ye or nay,
Yet sometime it shal fallen on a day
That falleth nat eft withinne a thousand yeer.
For certeinly oure appetites heer,
Be it of werre or pees, or hate or love,
Al is this reuled by the sighte above.

　　This mene I now by mighty Theseus,
That for to hunten is so desirus,
And namely at the grete hert in May,
That in his bed ther daweth him no day
That he nis clad and redy for to ride
With hunte and horn and houndes him biside.
For in his hunting hath he swich delit
That it is al his joye and appetit
To been himself the grete hertes bane,
For after Mars he serveth now Diane.

　　Cleer was the day, as I have toold er this,

And Theseus with alle joye and blis,
With his Ypolita, the faire queene,
And Emelye, clothed al in grene,
On hunting be they riden roially.
And to the grove that stood ful faste by,   830
In which ther was an hert, as men him tolde,
Duc Theseus the streighte wey hath holde.
And to the launde he rideth him ful right,
For thider was the hert wont have his flight,
And over a brook, and so forth on his weye.
This duc wol han a cours at him or tweye
With houndes swiche as that him list comaunde.
    And whan this duc was come unto the launde,
Under the sonne he looketh, and anon
He was war of Arcite and Palamon,   840
That foughten breme as it were bores two.
The brighte swerdes wenten to and fro
So hidously that with the leeste strook
It semed as it wolde felle an ook.
But what they were no thing he ne woot.
This duc his courser with his spores smoot,
And at a stert he was bitwix hem two,
And pulled out a swerd, and cride, 'Hoo!
Namoore, up peyne of lesinge of youre heed!
By mighty Mars, he shal anon be deed   850
That smiteth any strook that I may seen.
But telleth me what myster men ye been,
That been so hardy for to fighten heere
Withouten juge or oother officere,
As it were in a listes roially.'
    This Palamon answerde hastily,
And seyde, 'Sire, what nedeth wordes mo?

We have the deeth disserved bothe two.
Two woful wrecches been we, two caytyves,
That been encombred of oure owene lives;
And as thou art a rightful lord and juge,
Ne yif us neither mercy ne refuge,
But sle me first, for seinte charitee!
But sle my felawe eek as wel as me;
Or sle him first, for though thow knowest it lite,
This is thy mortal foo, this is Arcite,
That fro thy lond is banisshed on his heed,
For which he hath deserved to be deed.
For this is he that cam unto thy gate
And seyde that he highte Philostrate.
Thus hath he japed thee ful many a yer,
And thou hast maked him thy chief squier;
And this is he that loveth Emelye.
For sith the day is come that I shal die,
I make pleynly my confessioun
That I am thilke woful Palamoun
That hath thy prisoun broken wikkedly.
I am thy mortal foo, and it am I
That loveth so hoote Emelye the brighte
That I wol die present in hir sighte.
Wherfore I axe deeth and my juwise;
But sle my felawe in the same wise,
For bothe han we deserved to be slain.'
    This worthy duc answerde anon again
And seyde, 'This is a short conclusioun.
Youre owene mouth, by youre confessioun,
Hath dampned yow, and I wol it recorde;
It nedeth noght to pine yow with the corde.
Ye shal be deed, by mighty Mars the rede!'

The queene anon for verray wommanhede   890
Gan for to wepe, and so dide Emelye
And alle the ladies in the compaignye.
Greet pitee was it, as it thoughte hem alle,
That evere swich a chaunce sholde falle;
For gentil men they were of greet estaat,
And no thing but for love was this debaat;
And saugh hir blody woundes wide and soore,
And alle crieden, bothe lasse and moore,
'Have mercy, Lord, upon us wommen alle!'
And on hir bare knees adoun they falle,   900
And wolde have kist his feet ther as he stood;
Til at the laste aslaked was his mood,
For pitee renneth soone in gentil herte.
And though he first for ire quook and sterte,
He hath considered shortly, in a clause,
The trespas of hem bothe, and eek the cause,
And although that his ire hir gilt accused,
Yet in his resoun he hem bothe excused,
As thus: he thoghte wel that every man
Wol helpe himself in love, if that he kan,   910
And eek delivere himself out of prisoun.
And eek his herte hadde compassioun
Of wommen, for they wepen evere in oon;
And in his gentil herte he thoughte anon,
And softe unto himself he seyde, 'Fy
Upon a lord that wol have no mercy,
But been a leon, bothe in word and dede,
To hem that been in repentaunce and drede,
As wel as to a proud despitous man
That wol maintene that he first bigan.   920
That lord hath litel of discrecioun

That in swich cas kan no divisioun,
But weyeth pride and humblesse after oon.'
And shortly, whan his ire is thus agoon,
He gan to looken up with eyen lighte,
And spak thise same wordes al on highte:
    'The god of love, a, *benedicite!*
How mighty and how greet a lord is he!
Ayeyns his might ther gaineth none obstacles.
930   He may be cleped a god for his miracles;
For he kan maken, at his owene gyse,
Of everich herte as that him list divyse.
Lo heere this Arcite and this Palamoun,
That quitly weren out of my prisoun,
And mighte han lived in Thebes roially,
And witen I am hir mortal enemy,
And that hir deth lith in my might also;
And yet hath love, maugree hir eyen two,
Broght hem hider bothe for to die.
940   Now looketh, is nat that an heigh folye?
Who may been a fool, but if he love?
Bihoold, for Goddes sake that sit above,
Se how they blede! be they noght wel arrayed?
Thus hath hir lord, the god of love, ypayed
Hir wages and hir fees for hir servise!
And yet they wenen for to been ful wise
That serven love, for aught that may bifalle.
But this is yet the beste game of alle,
That she for whom they han this jolitee
950   Kan hem therfore as muche thank as me.
She woot namoore of al this hoote fare,
By God, than woot a cokkow or an hare!
But all moot ben assayed, hoot and coold;

A man moot ben a fool, or yong or oold—
I woot it by myself ful yore agon,
For in my time a servant was I oon.
And therfore, sin I knowe of loves peyne,
And woot hou soore it kan a man distreyne,
As he that hath ben caught ofte in his laas,
I yow foryeve al hoolly this trespaas,   960
At requeste of the queene, that kneleth heere,
And eek of Emelye, my suster deere.
And ye shul bothe anon unto me swere
That nevere mo ye shal my contree dere,
Ne make werre upon me night ne day,
But been my freendes in all that ye may.
I yow foryeve this trespas every deel.'
And they him sworen his axing faire and weel,
And him of lordshipe and of mercy preyde,
And he hem graunteth grace, and thus he seyde: 970
    'To speke of roial linage and richesse,
Though that she were a queene or a princesse,
Ech of you bothe is worthy, doutelees,
To wedden whan time is, but nathelees
I speke as for my suster Emelye,
For whom ye have this strif and jalousye.
Ye woot yourself she may nat wedden two
Atones, though ye fighten everemo.
That oon of you, al be him looth or lief,
He moot go pipen in an ivy leef;   980
This is to seyn, she may nat now han bothe,
Al be ye never so jalouse ne so wrothe.
And forthy I yow putte in this degree,
That ech of yow shal have his destinee
As him is shape, and herkneth in what wise;

113

Lo heere youre ende of that I shal devyse.
My wil is this, for plat conclusioun,
Withouten any repplicacioun—
If that you liketh, take it for the beste:
That everich of you shal goon where him leste
Frely, withouten raunson or daunger;
And this day fifty wykes, fer ne ner,
Everich of you shal bringe an hundred knightes
Armed for listes up at alle rightes,
Al redy to darreyne hire by bataille.
And this bihote I yow withouten faille,
Upon my trouthe, and as I am a knight,
That wheither of yow bothe that hath might—
This is to seyn, that wheither he or thow
May with his hundred, as I spak of now,
Sleen his contrarie or out of listes drive—
Thanne shal I yeve Emelya to wyve
To whom that Fortune yeveth so fair a grace.
The listes shal I maken in this place,
And God so wisly on my soule rewe,
As I shal evene juge been and trewe.
Ye shul noon oother ende with me maken,
That oon of yow ne shal be deed or taken.
And if yow thinketh this is weel ysaid,
Seyeth youre avis, and holdeth you apayd.
This is youre ende and youre conclusioun.'

Who looketh lightly now but Palamoun?
Who springeth up for joye but Arcite?
Who kouthe telle, or who kouthe it endite,
The joye that is maked in the place
Whan Theseus hath doon so fair a grace?
But doun on knees wente every maner wight,

And thonked him with al hir herte and might,
And namely the Thebans often sithe.
And thus with good hope and with herte blithe   1020
They taken hir leve, and homward gonne they ride
To Thebes, with his olde walles wide.

PART III

I trowe men wolde deme it necligence
If I foryete to tellen the dispence
Of Theseus, that gooth so bisily
To maken up the listes roially,
That swich a noble theatre as it was
I dar wel seyen in this world ther nas.
The circuit a mile was aboute,
Walled of stoon, and diched al withoute.   1030
Round was the shap, in manere of compas,
Ful of degrees, the heighte of sixty pas,
That whan a man was set on o degree
He letted nat his felawe for to see.

Estward ther stood a gate of marbul whit,
Westward right swich another in the opposit.
And shortly to concluden, swich a place
Was noon in erthe, as in so litel space;
For in the lond ther was no crafty man
That geometrie or ars-metrike kan,   1040
Ne portreyour, ne kervere of images,
That Theseus ne yaf him mete and wages,
The theatre for to maken and devyse.
And for to doon his rite and sacrifise,
He estward hath, upon the gate above,
In worshipe of Venus, goddesse of love,

Doon make an auter and an oratorie;
And on the gate westward, in memorie
Of Mars, he maked hath right swich another,
1050 That coste largely of gold a fother.
And northward, in a touret on the wal,
Of alabastre whit and reed coral,
An oratorie, riche for to see,
In worshipe of Diane of chastitee,
Hath Theseus doon wroght in noble wise.

But yet hadde I foryeten to devyse
The noble kerving and the portreitures,
The shap, the contenaunce, and the figures,
That weren in thise oratories thre.
1060 First in the temple of Venus maystow se
Wroght on the wal, ful pitous to biholde,
The broken slepes and the sikes colde,
The sacred teeris and the waymentinge,
The firy strokes of the desiringe
That loves servantz in this lyf enduren;
The othes that hir covenantz assuren;
Plesaunce and Hope, Desir, Foolhardinesse,
Beautee and Youthe, Bauderie, Richesse,
Charmes and Force, Lesinges, Flaterye,
1070 Despense, Bisynesse; and Jalousye,
That wered of yelewe goooldes a gerland,
And a cokkow sittinge on hir hand;
Festes, instrumentz, caroles, daunces,
Lust and array, and alle the circumstaunces
Of love which that I rekned and rekne shal,
By ordre weren peynted on the wal,
And mo than I kan make of mencioun.
For soothly al the mount of Citheroun,

Ther Venus hath hir principal dwellinge,
Was shewed on the wal in portreyinge,   1080
With al the gardyn and the lustinesse.
Nat was foryeten the porter, Idelnesse,
Ne Narcisus the faire of yore agon,
Ne yet the folye of king Salomon,
Ne yet the grete strengthe of Ercules,
Th'enchauntementz of Medea and Circes,
Ne of Turnus with the hardy fiers corage,
The riche Cresus, kaytyf in servage.
Thus may ye seen that wisdom ne richesse,
Beautee ne sleighte, strengthe ne hardinesse,   1090
Ne may with Venus holde champartie,
For as hir list the world than may she gye.
Lo, alle thise folk so caught were in hir las,
Til they for wo ful ofte seyde 'allas!'
Suffiseth heere ensamples oon or two,
And though I koude rekene a thousand mo.

The statue of Venus, glorious for to se,
Was naked, fletinge in the large see,
And fro the navele doun al covered was
With wawes grene, and brighte as any glas.   1100
A citole in hir right hand hadde she,
And on hir heed, ful semely for to se,
A rose gerland, fressh and wel smellinge;
Above hir heed hir dowves flikeringe.
Biforn hire stood hir sone Cupido;
Upon his shuldres winges hadde he two,
And blind he was, as it is often seene;
A bowe he bar and arwes brighte and kene.

Why sholde I noght as wel eek telle yow al
The portreiture that was upon the wal   1110

117

Withinne the temple of mighty Mars the rede?
Al peynted was the wal, in lengthe and brede,
Lyk to the estres of the grisly place
That highte the grete temple of Mars in Trace,
In thilke colde, frosty regioun
Ther as Mars hath his soverein mansioun.

    First on the wal was peynted a forest,
In which ther dwelleth neither man ne best,
With knotty, knarry, bareyne trees olde,
Of stubbes sharpe and hidouse to biholde,
In which ther ran a rumbel in a swough,
As though a storm sholde bresten every bough.
And dounward from an hille, under a bente,
Ther stood the temple of Mars armipotente,
Wroght al of burned steel, of which the entree
Was long and streit, and gastly for to see.
And therout came a rage and swich a veze
That it made al the gate for to rese.
The northren light in at the dores shoon,
For windowe on the wal ne was ther noon
Thurgh which men mighten any light discerne.
The dore was al of adamant eterne,
Yclenched overthwart and endelong
With iren tough; and for to make it strong,
Every piler, the temple to sustene,
Was tonne-greet, of iren bright and shene.

    Ther saugh I first the derke imagining
Of Felonye, and al the compassing;
The crueel Ire, reed as any gleede;
The pykepurs, and eek the pale Drede;
The smilere with the knyf under the cloke;
The shepne brenninge with the blake smoke;

The tresoun of the mordringe in the bedde;
The open werre, with woundes al bibledde;
Contek, with blody knyf and sharp manace.
Al ful of chirking was that sory place.
The sleere of himself yet saugh I ther—
His herte-blood hath bathed al his heer;
The nail ydriven in the shode a-night;
The colde deeth, with mouth gaping upright.   1150
Amiddes of the temple sat Meschaunce,
With disconfort and sory contenaunce.
Yet saugh I Woodnesse, laughinge in his rage,
Armed Compleint, Outhees, and fiers Outrage;
The careyne in the busk, with throte ycorve;
A thousand slain, and nat of qualm ystorve;
The tiraunt, with the pray by force yraft;
The toun destroyed, ther was no thing laft.
Yet saugh I brent the shippes hoppesteres;
The hunte strangled with the wilde beres;   1160
The sowe freten the child right in the cradel;
The cook yscalded, for al his longe ladel.
Noght was foryeten by the infortune of Marte
The cartere overriden with his carte:
Under the wheel ful lowe he lay adoun.
Ther were also, of Martes divisioun,
The barbour, and the bocher, and the smith,
That forgeth sharpe swerdes on his stith.
And al above, depeynted in a tour,
Saugh I Conquest sittinge in greet honour,   1170
With the sharpe swerd over his heed
Hanginge by a soutil twines threed.
Depeynted was the slaughtre of Julius,
Of grete Nero, and of Antonius;

Al be that thilke time they were unborn,
Yet was hir deth depeynted ther-biforn
By manasinge of Mars, right by figure.
So was it shewed in that portreiture,
As is depeynted in the sterres above
Who shal be slain or elles deed for love.
Suffiseth oon ensample in stories olde;
I may nat rekene hem alle though I wolde.

The statue of Mars upon a carte stood
Armed, and looked grim as he were wood;
And over his heed ther shinen two figures
Of sterres, that been cleped in scriptures
That oon Puella, that oother Rubeus—
This god of armes was arrayed thus.
A wolf ther stood biforn him at his feet
With eyen rede, and of a man he eet;
With soutil pencel depeynted was this storie
In redoutinge of Mars and of his glorie.

Now to the temple of Diane the chaste,
As shortly as I kan, I wol me haste,
To telle yow al the descripsioun.
Depeynted been the walles up and doun
Of hunting and of shamefast chastitee.
Ther saugh I how woful Calistopee,
Whan that Diane agreved was with here,
Was turned from a womman til a bere,
And after was she maad the loode-sterre;
Thus was it peynted, I kan sey yow no ferre.
Hir sone is eek a sterre, as men may see.
Ther saugh I Dane, yturned til a tree—
I mene nat the goddesse Diane,
But Penneus doghter, which that highte Dane.

Ther saugh I Attheon an hert ymaked,
For vengeaunce that he saugh Diane al naked;
I saugh how that his houndes have him caught
And freeten him, for that they knewe him naught. 1210
Yet peynted was a litel forther moor
How Atthalante hunted the wilde boor,
And Meleagre, and many another mo,
For which Diane wroghte him care and wo.
Ther saugh I many another wonder storie,
The which me list nat drawen to memorie.

This goddesse on an hert ful hye seet,
With smale houndes al aboute hir feet;
And undernethe hir feet she hadde a moone—
Wexinge it was and sholde wanye soone.   1220
In gaude grene hir statue clothed was,
With bowe in honde, and arwes in a cas.
Hir eyen caste she ful lowe adoun
Ther Pluto hath his derke regioun.
A womman travaillinge was hire biforn;
But for hir child so longe was unborn,
Ful pitously Lucina gan she calle,
And seyde, 'Help, for thou mayst best of alle!'
Wel koude he peynten lifly that it wroghte;
With many a florin he the hewes boghte.   1230

Now been thise listes maad, and Theseus,
That at his grete cost arrayed thus
The temples and the theatre every deel,
Whan it was doon, him liked wonder weel.
But stynte I wole of Theseus a lite,
And speke of Palamon and of Arcite.

The day approcheth of hir retourninge,
That everich sholde an hundred knightes bringe

The bataille to darreyne, as I yow tolde.
1240 And til Atthenes, hir covenant for to holde,
Hath everich of hem broght an hundred knightes,
Wel armed for the werre at alle rightes.
And sikerly ther trowed many a man
That nevere, sithen that the world bigan,
As for to speke of knighthod of hir hond,
As fer as God hath maked see or lond,
Nas of so fewe so noble a compaignye.
For every wight that lovede chivalrye,
And wolde his thankes han a passant name,
1250 Hath preyed that he mighte been of that game;
And wel was him that therto chosen was.
For if ther fille tomorwe swich a cas,
Ye knowen wel that every lusty knight
That loveth paramours and hath his might,
Were it in Engelond or elleswhere,
They wolde, hir thankes, wilnen to be there—
To fighte for a lady, *benedicitee*,
It were a lusty sighte for to see.
    And right so ferden they with Palamon.
1260 With him ther wenten knightes many on;
Som wol ben armed in an haubergeoun,
And in a brestplate and a light gypoun;
And som wol have a paire plates large;
And som wol have a Pruce sheeld or a targe;
Som wol ben armed on his legges weel,
And have an ax, and som a mace of steel—
Ther is no newe gyse that it nas old.
Armed were they, as I have yow told,
Everich after his opinioun.
1270   Ther maistow seen cominge with Palamoun

122

Lygurge himself, the grete king of Trace.
Blak was his berd and manly was his face;
The cercles of his eyen in his heed,
They gloweden bitwixen yelow and reed,
And lik a grifphon looked he aboute,
With kempe heeris on his browes stoute;
His lymes grete, his brawnes harde and stronge,
His shuldres brode, his armes rounde and longe;
And as the gyse was in his contree,
Ful hye upon a chaar of gold stood he,   1280
With foure white boles in the trais.
In stede of cote-armure over his harnais,
With nailes yelewe and brighte as any gold,
He hadde a beres skin, col-blak for old.
His longe heer was kembd bihinde his bak;
As any ravenes fethere it shoon for blak;
A wrethe of gold, arm-greet, of huge wighte,
Upon his heed, set ful of stones brighte,
Of fine rubies and of diamauntz.
Aboute his chaar ther wenten white alauntz,   1290
Twenty and mo, as grete as any steer,
To hunten at the leoun or the deer,
And folwed him with mosel faste ybounde,
Colered of gold, and tourettes filed rounde.
An hundred lordes hadde he in his route,
Armed ful wel, with hertes stierne and stoute.
   With Arcita, in stories as men finde,
The grete Emetreus, the king of Inde,
Upon a steede bay trapped in steel,
Covered in clooth of gold, diapred weel,   1300
Cam ridinge lyk the god of armes, Mars.
His cote-armure was of clooth of Tars

Couched with perles white and rounde and grete;
His sadel was of brend gold newe ybete;
A mantelet upon his shulder hanginge,
Bret-ful of rubies rede as fyr sparklinge;
His crispe heer lyk ringes was yronne,
And that was yelow, and glitered as the sonne.
His nose was heigh, his eyen bright citrin,
His lippes rounde, his colour was sangwin;
A fewe frakenes in his face yspreynd,
Bitwixen yelow and somdel blak ymeynd;
And as a leon he his looking caste.
Of five and twenty yeer his age I caste.
His berd was wel bigonne for to springe;
His vois was as a trompe thonderinge.
Upon his heed he wered of laurer grene
A gerland, fressh and lusty for to sene.
Upon his hand he bar for his deduyt
An egle tame, as any lilye whyt.
An hundred lordes hadde he with him there,
Al armed, save hir heddes, in al hir gere,
Ful richely in alle maner thinges.
For trusteth wel that dukes, erles, kinges
Were gadered in this noble compaignye,
For love and for encrees of chivalrye.
Aboute this king ther ran on every part
Ful many a tame leon and leopart.
And in this wise thise lordes, alle and some,
Been on the Sonday to the citee come
Aboute prime, and in the toun alight.

This Theseus, this duc, this worthy knight,
Whan he had broght hem into his citee,
And inned hem, everich at his degree,

He festeth hem, and dooth so greet labour
To esen hem and doon hem al honour,
That yet men wenen that no mannes wit
Of noon estaat ne koude amenden it.

The minstralcye, the service at the feeste,
The grete yiftes to the meeste and leeste,   1340
The riche array of Theseus paleys,
Ne who sat first ne last upon the deys,
What ladies fairest been or best daunsinge,
Or which of hem kan dauncen best and singe,
Ne who moost felingly speketh of love;
What haukes sitten on the perche above,
What houndes liggen on the floor adoun—
Of al this make I now no mencioun,
But al th'effect, that thinketh me the beste.
Now cometh the point, and herkneth if yow leste. 1350

The Sonday night, er day bigan to springe,
Whan Palamon the larke herde singe,
(Although it nere nat day by houres two,
Yet song the larke) and Palamon right tho
With hooly herte and with an heigh corage,
He roos to wenden on his pilgrimage
Unto the blisful Citherea benigne—
I mene Venus, honurable and digne.
And in hir houre he walketh forth a pas
Unto the listes ther hire temple was,   1360
And doun he kneleth, and with humble cheere
And herte soor he seyde as ye shal heere:

'Faireste of faire, O lady myn, Venus,
Doughter to Jove, and spouse of Vulcanus,
Thow gladere of the mount of Citheron,
For thilke love thow haddest to Adoon,

Have pitee of my bittre teeris smerte,
And taak myn humble preyere at thyn herte.
Allas! I ne have no langage to telle

1370 Th'effectes ne the tormentz of myn helle;
Myn herte may mine harmes nat biwreye;
I am so confus that I kan noght seye
But, "Mercy, lady bright, that knowest weele
My thought and seest what harmes that I feele!"
Considere al this and rewe upon my soore,
As wisly as I shal for everemoore,
Emforth my might, thy trewe servant be,
And holden werre alwey with chastitee.
That make I myn avow, so ye me helpe.

1380 I kepe noght of armes for to yelpe,
Ne I ne axe nat tomorwe to have victorie,
Ne renoun in this cas, ne veyne glorie
Of pris of armes blowen up and doun;
But I wolde have fully possessioun
Of Emelye, and die in thy servise.
Find thow the manere hou, and in what wise:
I recche nat but it may bettre be
To have victorie of hem, or they of me,
So that I have my lady in mine armes.

1390 For though so be that Mars is god of armes,
Youre vertu is so greet in hevene above
That if yow list I shal wel have my love.
Thy temple wol I worshipe everemo,
And on thyn auter, where I ride or go,
I wol doon sacrifice and fires beete.
And if ye wol nat so, my lady sweete,
Thanne preye I thee tomorwe with a spere
That Arcita me thurgh the herte bere.

Thanne rekke I noght, whan I have lost my lyf,
Though that Arcita winne hire to his wyf.   1400
This is th'effect and ende of my preyere:
Yif me my love, thow blisful lady deere.'

    Whan the orison was doon of Palamon,
His sacrifice he dide, and that anon,
Ful pitously, with alle circumstaunces,
Al telle I noght as now his observaunces;
But atte laste the statue of Venus shook,
And made a signe, wherby that he took
That his preyere accepted was that day.
For thogh the signe shewed a delay,   1410
Yet wiste he wel that graunted was his boone;
And with glad herte he wente him hoom ful soone.

    The thridde houre inequal that Palamon
Bigan to Venus temple for to gon,
Up roos the sonne, and up roos Emelye
And to the temple of Diane gan hie.
Hir maidens, that she thider with hire ladde,
Ful redily with hem the fyr they hadde,
Th'encens, the clothes, and the remenant al
That to the sacrifice longen shal;   1420
The hornes fulle of meeth, as was the gyse:
Ther lakked noght to doon hir sacrifise.
Smokinge the temple, ful of clothes faire,
This Emelye, with herte debonaire,
Hir body wessh with water of a welle.
But hou she dide hir rite I dar nat telle,
But it be any thing in general;
And yet it were a game to heeren al.
To him that meneth wel it were no charge;
But it is good a man been at his large.   1430

127

Hir brighte heer was kembd, untressed al;
A coroune of a grene ook cerial
Upon hir heed was set ful fair and meete.
Two fires on the auter gan she beete,
And dide hir thinges, as men may biholde
In Stace of Thebes and thise bookes olde.
Whan kindled was the fyr, with pitous cheere
Unto Diane she spak as ye may heere:
  'O chaste goddesse of the wodes grene,

1440   To whom bothe hevene and erthe and see is sene,
Queene of the regne of Pluto derk and lowe,
Goddesse of maidens, that myn herte hast knowe
Ful many a yeer, and woost what I desire,
As keepe me fro thy vengeaunce and thyn ire,
That Attheon aboughte cruelly.
Chaste goddesse, wel wostow that I
Desire to ben a maiden al my lyf,
Ne nevere wol I be no love ne wyf.
I am, thow woost, yet of thy compaignye,

1450   A maide, and love huntinge and venerye,
And for to walken in the wodes wilde,
And noght to ben a wyf and be with childe.
Noght wol I knowe compaignye of man.
Now help me, lady, sith ye may and kan,
For tho thre formes that thou hast in thee.
And Palamon, that hath swich love to me,
And eek Arcite, that loveth me so soore,
(This grace I preye thee withoute moore)
As sende love and pees bitwixe hem two,

1460   And fro me turne awey hir hertes so
That al hire hoote love and hir desir,
And al hir bisy torment, and hir fir

Be queynt, or turned in another place.
And if so be thou wolt nat do me grace,
Or if my destinee be shapen so
That I shal nedes have oon of hem two,
As sende me him that moost desireth me.
Bihoold, goddesse of clene chastitee,
The bittre teeris that on my chekes falle.
Sin thou art maide and kepere of us alle,   1470
My maidenhede thou kepe and wel conserve,
And whil I live, a maide I wol thee serve.'
    The fires brenne upon the auter cleere,
Whil Emelye was thus in hir preyere.
But sodeynly she saugh a sighte queynte,
For right anon oon of the fires queynte,
And quiked again, and after that anon
That oother fyr was queynt and al agon;
And as it queynte it made a whistelinge,
As doon thise wete brondes in hir brenninge,   1480
And at the brondes ende out ran anon
As it were blody dropes many oon;
For which so soore agast was Emelye
That she was wel ny mad, and gan to crye,
For she ne wiste what it signified;
But oonly for the feere thus hath she cried,
And weep that it was pitee for to heere.
And therwithal Diane gan appeere,
With bowe in honde, right as an hunteresse,
And seyde, 'Doghter, stynt thyn hevinesse.   1490
Among the goddes hye it is affermed,
And by eterne word writen and confermed,
Thou shalt ben wedded unto oon of tho
That han for thee so muchel care and wo;

But unto which of hem I may nat telle.
Farwel, for I ne may no lenger dwelle.
The fires which that on myn auter brenne
Shulle thee declaren, er that thou go henne,
Thyn aventure of love, as in this cas.'
1500 And with that word, the arwes in the caas
Of the goddesse clateren faste and ringe,
And forth she wente, and made a vanisshinge;
For which this Emelye astoned was,
And seyde, 'What amounteth this, allas?
I putte me in thy proteccioun,
Diane, and in thy disposicioun.'
And hoom she goth anon the nexte weye.
This is th'effect; ther is namoore to seye.

 The nexte houre of Mars folwinge this,
1510 Arcite unto the temple walked is
Of fierse Mars to doon his sacrifise,
With alle the rites of his payen wise.
With pitous herte and heigh devocioun
Right thus to Mars he seyde his orisoun:
 'O stronge god, that in the regnes colde
Of Trace honoured art and lord yholde,
And hast in every regne and every lond
Of armes al the bridel in thyn hond,
And hem fortunest as thee list devyse,
1520 Accepte of me my pitous sacrifise.
If so be that my youthe may deserve,
And that my might be worthy for to serve
Thy godhede, that I may been oon of thine,
Thanne preye I thee to rewe upon my pine.
For thilke peyne and thilke hoote fir
In which thow whilom brendest for desir,

Whan that thow usedest the beautee
Of faire, yonge, fresshe Venus free,
And haddest hire in armes at thy wille—
Although thee ones on a time misfille,   1530
Whan Vulcanus hadde caught thee in his las,
And foond thee ligginge by his wyf, allas!—
For thilke sorwe that was in thyn herte,
Have routhe as wel upon my peynes smerte.
I am yong and unkonninge, as thow woost,
And, as I trowe, with love offended moost
That evere was any lives creature;
For she that dooth me al this wo endure
Ne reccheth nevere wher I sinke or fleete.
And wel I woot, er she me mercy heete,   1540
I moot with strengthe winne hire in the place,
And, wel I woot, withouten help or grace
Of thee, ne may my strengthe noght availle.
Thanne help me, lord, tomorwe in my bataille,
For thilke fyr that whilom brente thee,
As wel as thilke fyr now brenneth me,
And do that I tomorwe have victorie.
Myn be the travaille and thyn be the glorie!
Thy soverein temple wol I moost honouren
Of any place, and alwey moost labouren   1550
In thy plesaunce and in thy craftes stronge,
And in thy temple I wol my baner honge
And alle the armes of my compaignye;
And everemo, unto that day I die,
Eterne fir I wol bifore thee finde.
And eek to this avow I wol me binde:
My beerd, myn heer, that hongeth long adoun,
That nevere yet ne felte offensioun

Of rasour nor of shere, I wol thee yive,
1560 And ben thy trewe servant whil I live.
Now, lord, have routhe upon my sorwes soore;
Yif me victorie, I aske thee namoore.'

The preyere stynt of Arcita the stronge,
The ringes on the temple dore that honge,
And eek the dores, clatereden ful faste,
Of which Arcita somwhat him agaste.
The fires brenden upon the auter brighte,
That it gan al the temple for to lighte;
A sweete smel the ground anon up yaf,
1570 And Arcita anon his hand up haf
And moore encens into the fyr he caste,
With othere rites mo; and atte laste
The statue of Mars bigan his hauberk ringe;
And with that soun he herde a murmuringe
Ful lowe and dim, and seyde thus, 'Victorie!'
For which he yaf to Mars honour and glorie.
And thus with joye and hope wel to fare
Arcite anon unto his in is fare,
As fain as fowel is of the brighte sonne.
1580 And right anon swich strif ther is bigonne,
For thilke graunting, in the hevene above,
Bitwixe Venus, the goddesse of love,
And Mars, the stierne god armipotente,
That Juppiter was bisy it to stente;
Til that the pale Saturnus the colde,
That knew so manye of aventures olde,
Foond in his olde experience an art
That he ful soone hath plesed every part.
As sooth is seyd, elde hath greet avantage;
1590 In elde is bothe wisdom and usage;

Men may the olde atrenne, and noght atrede.
Saturne anon, to stynten strif and drede,
Al be it that it is again his kinde,
Of al this strif he gan remedie finde.
  'My deere doghter Venus,' quod Saturne,
'My cours, that hath so wide for to turne,
Hath moore power than woot any man.
Myn is the drenching in the see so wan;
Myn is the prison in the derke cote;
Myn is the strangling and hanging by the throte,   1600
The murmure and the cherles rebelling,
The groininge, and the privee empoisoning;
I do vengeance and pleyn correccioun,
Whil I dwelle in the signe of the leoun.
Myn is the ruine of the hye halles,
The fallinge of the toures and of the walles
Upon the minour or the carpenter.
I slow Sampsoun, shakinge the piler;
And mine be the maladies colde,
The derke tresons, and the castes olde;   1610
My looking is the fader of pestilence.
Now weep namoore, I shal doon diligence
That Palamon, that is thyn owene knight,
Shal have his lady, as thou hast him hight.
Though Mars shal helpe his knight, yet nathelees
Bitwixe yow ther moot be som time pees,
Al be ye noght of o compleccioun,
That causeth al day swich divisioun.
I am thyn aiel, redy at thy wille;
Weep now namoore, I wol thy lust fulfille.'   1620
  Now wol I stynten of the goddes above,
Of Mars, and of Venus, goddesse of love,

And telle yow as pleynly as I kan
The grete effect, for which that I bigan.

PART IV

Greet was the feeste in Atthenes that day,
And eek the lusty seson of that May
Made every wight to been in swich plesaunce
That al that Monday justen they and daunce,
And spenden it in Venus heigh servise.
1630   But by the cause that they sholde rise
Eerly, for to seen the grete fight,
Unto hir reste wenten they at night.
And on the morwe, whan that day gan springe,
Of hors and harneys noise and clateringe
Ther was in hostelries al aboute;
And to the paleys rood ther many a route
Of lordes upon steedes and palfreys.
Ther maystow seen devisinge of harneys
So unkouth and so riche, and wroght so weel
1640   Of goldsmithrye, of browdinge, and of steel;
The sheeldes brighte, testeres, and trappures,
Gold-hewen helmes, hauberkes, cote-armures;
Lordes in parementz on hir courseres,
Knightes of retenue, and eek squieres
Nailinge the speres, and helmes bokelinge;
Gigginge of sheeldes, with layneres lacinge
(There as nede is they weren no thing idel);
The fomy steedes on the golden bridel
Gnawinge, and faste the armurers also
1650   With file and hamer prikinge to and fro;
Yemen on foote, and communes many oon

With shorte staves, thikke as they may goon;
Pipes, trompes, nakers, clariounes,
That in the bataille blowen blody sounes;
The paleys ful of peple up and doun,
Heere thre, ther ten, holdinge hir questioun,
Divininge of thise Thebane knightes two.
Somme seyden thus, somme seyde 'it shal be so';
Somme helden with him with the blake berd,
Somme with the balled, somme with the thikke herd; 1660
Somme seyde he looked grimme, and he wolde fighte;
'He hath a sparth of twenty pound of wighte.'
Thus was the halle ful of divininge,
Longe after that the sonne gan to springe.

The grete Theseus, that of his sleep awaked
With minstralcie and noise that was maked,
Heeld yet the chambre of his paleys riche,
Til that the Thebane knightes, bothe yliche
Honured, were into the paleys fet.
Duc Theseus was at a window set,   1670
Arrayed right as he were a god in trone.
The peple preesseth thiderward ful soone
Him for to seen, and doon heigh reverence,
And eek to herkne his heste and his sentence.
An heraud on a scaffold made an 'Oo!'
Til al the noise of peple was ydo,
And whan he saugh the peple of noise al stille,
Tho shewed he the mighty dukes wille.

'The lord hath of his heigh discrecioun
Considered that it were destruccioun   1680
To gentil blood to fighten in the gyse
Of mortal bataille now in this emprise.
Wherfore, to shapen that they shal nat die,

He wol his firste purpos modifye.
No man therfore, up peyne of los of lyf,
No maner shot, ne polax, ne short knyf
Into the listes sende or thider bringe;
Ne short swerd, for to stoke with point bitinge,
No man ne drawe ne bere it by his side.
1690 Ne no man shal unto his felawe ride
But o cours, with a sharpe ygrounde spere;
Foyne, if him list, on foote, himself to were.
And he that is at meschief shal be take
And noght slain, but be broght unto the stake
That shal ben ordeyned on either side;
But thider he shal by force, and there abide.
And if so falle the chieftain be take
On outher side, or elles sleen his make,
No lenger shal the turneyinge laste.
1700 God spede you! gooth forth, and ley on faste!
With long swerd and with maces fighteth youre fille.
Gooth now youre wey, this is the lordes wille.'

The vois of peple touchede the hevene,
So loude cride they with murie stevene,
'God save swich a lord, that is so good,
He wilneth no destruccion of blood!'
Up goon the trompes and the melodye,
And to the listes rit the compaignye,
By ordinance, thurghout the citee large,
1710 Hanged with clooth of gold, and nat with sarge.
Ful lik a lord this noble duc gan ride,
Thise two Thebans upon either side;
And after rood the queene, and Emelye,
And after that another compaignye
Of oon and oother, after hir degree.

And thus they passen thurghout the citee,
And to the listes come they by time.
It nas nat of the day yet fully prime
Whan set was Theseus ful riche and hye,
Ypolita the queene, and Emelye,   1720
And othere ladys in degrees aboute.
Unto the seetes preesseth al the route.
And westward, thurgh the gates under Marte,
Arcite, and eek the hondred of his parte,
With baner reed is entred right anon;
And in that selve moment Palamon
Is under Venus, estward in the place,
With baner whyt, and hardy chiere and face.
In al the world, to seken up and doun,
So evene, withouten variacioun,   1730
Ther nere swiche compaignies tweye;
For ther was noon so wys that koude seye
That any hadde of oother avauntage
Of worthinesse, ne of estaat, ne age,
So evene were they chosen, for to gesse.
And in two renges faire they hem dresse.
Whan that hir names rad were everichon,
That in hir nombre gyle were ther noon,
Tho were the gates shet, and cried was loude:
'Do now youre devoir, yonge knightes proude!'   1740
    The heraudes lefte hir priking up and doun;
Now ringen trompes loude and clarioun.
Ther is namoore to seyn, but west and est
In goon the speres ful sadly in arrest;
In gooth the sharpe spore into the side.
Ther seen men who kan juste and who kan ride;
Ther shiveren shaftes upon sheeldes thikke:

He feeleth thurgh the herte-spoon the prikke;
Up springen speres twenty foot on highte.
1750 Out goon the swerdes as the silver brighte;
The helmes they tohewen and toshrede;
Out brest the blood with stierne stremes rede;
With mighty maces the bones they tobreste.
He thurgh the thikkeste of the throng gan threste;
Ther stomblen steedes stronge, and doun gooth al;
He rolleth under foot as dooth a bal;
He foyneth on his feet with his tronchoun,
And he him hurtleth with his hors adoun;
He thurgh the body is hurt and sithen take,
1760 Maugree his heed, and broght unto the stake:
As forward was, right there he moste abide.
Another lad is on that oother side.
And some time dooth hem Theseus to reste,
Hem to refresshe and drinken, if hem leste.
Ful ofte a day han thise Thebanes two
Togidre ymet, and wroght his felawe wo;
Unhorsed hath ech oother of hem tweye.
Ther nas no tigre in the vale of Galgopheye,
Whan that hir whelp is stole whan it is lite,
1770 So crueel on the hunte as is Arcite
For jelous herte upon this Palamon.
Ne in Belmarye ther nis so fel leon,
That hunted is, or for his hunger wood,
Ne of his praye desireth so the blood,
As Palamon to sleen his foo Arcite.
The jelous strokes on hir helmes bite;
Out renneth blood on bothe hir sides rede.
　Som time an ende ther is of every dede.
For er the sonne unto the reste wente,

The stronge king Emetreus gan hente   1780
This Palamon, as he faught with Arcite,
And made his swerd depe in his flessh to bite;
And by the force of twenty is he take
Unyolden, and ydrawe unto the stake.
And in the rescus of this Palamoun
The stronge king Lygurge is born adoun,
And king Emetreus, for al his strengthe,
Is born out of his sadel a swerdes lengthe,
So hitte him Palamoun er he were take;
But al for noght, he was broght to the stake.   1790
His hardy herte mighte him helpe naught:
He moste abide whan that he was caught,
By force and eek by composicioun.

Who sorweth now but woful Palamoun,
That moot namoore goon again to fighte?
And whan that Theseus hadde seyn this sighte,
Unto the folk that foghten thus echon
He cryde, 'Hoo! namoore, for it is doon.
I wol be trewe juge, and no partie.
Arcite of Thebes shal have Emelie,   1800
That by his fortune hath hire faire ywonne.'
Anon ther is a noise of peple bigonne
For joye of this, so loude and heighe withalle,
It semed that the listes sholde falle.

What kan now faire Venus doon above?
What seith she now? What dooth this queene of love,
But wepeth so, for wantinge of hir wille,
Til that hir teeres in the listes fille?
She seyde, 'I am ashamed, douteless.'

Saturnus seyde, 'Doghter, hoold thy pees!   1810
Mars hath his wille, his knight hath al his boone,

And, by myn heed, thow shalt been esed soone.'
The trompours, with the loude minstralcie,
The heraudes, that ful loude yelle and crie,
Been in hire wele for joye of daun Arcite.
But herkneth me, and stynteth noise a lite,
Which a miracle ther bifel anon.

This fierse Arcite hath of his helm ydon,
And on a courser, for to shewe his face,
1820 He priketh endelong the large place
Lokinge upward upon this Emelye;
And she again him caste a freendlich ye
(For wommen, as to speken in comune,
They folwen alle the favour of Fortune)
And was al his chiere, as in his herte.

Out of the ground a furie infernal sterte,
From Pluto sent at requeste of Saturne,
For which his hors for fere gan to turne,
And leep aside, and foundred as he leep;
1830 And er that Arcite may taken keep,
He pighte him on the pomel of his heed,
That in the place he lay as he were deed,
His brest tobrosten with his sadel-bowe.
As blak he lay as any cole or crowe,
So was the blood yronnen in his face.
Anon he was yborn out of the place,
With herte soor, to Theseus paleys.
Tho was he korven out of his harneys,
And in a bed ybrought ful faire and blyve;
1840 For he was yet in memorie and alive,
And alwey cryinge after Emelye.

Duc Theseus, with al his compaignye,
Is comen hoom to Atthenes his citee

With alle blisse and greet solempnitee.
Al be it that this aventure was falle,
He nolde noght disconforten hem alle.
Men seyde eek that Arcite shal nat die;
He shal been heeled of his maladye.
And of another thing they weren as fain,
That of hem alle was ther noon yslain,   1850
Al were they soore yhurt, and namely oon,
That with a spere was thirled his brest boon.
To othere woundes and to broken armes
Somme hadden salves and somme hadden charmes;
Fermacies of herbes and eek save
They dronken, for they wolde hir lymes have.
For which this noble duc, as he wel kan,
Conforteth and honoureth every man,
And made revel al the longe night
Unto the straunge lordes, as was right.   1860
Ne ther was holden no disconfitinge
But as a justes or a tourneyinge;
For soothly ther was no disconfiture.
For falling nis nat but an aventure,
Ne to be lad by force unto the stake
Unyolden, and with twenty knightes take,
O persone allone, withouten mo,
And haried forth by arme, foot, and too,
And eke his steede driven forth with staves
With footmen, bothe yemen and eek knaves—   1870
It nas arretted him no vileynye;
Ther may no man clepen it cowardye.
For which anon duc Theseus leet crye,
To stynten alle rancour and envye,
The gree as wel of o side as of oother,

141

And either side ylik as ootheres brother;
And yaf hem yiftes after hir degree,
And fully heeld a feeste dayes three,
And conveyed the kinges worthily
1880   Out of his toun a journee largely.
And hoom wente every man the righte way.
Ther was namoore but 'Fare wel, have good day!'
Of this bataille I wol namoore endite,
But speke of Palamon and of Arcite.

   Swelleth the brest of Arcite, and the soore
Encreesseth at his herte moore and moore.
The clothered blood, for any lechecraft,
Corrupteth and is in his bouk ylaft,
That neither veine-blood, ne ventusinge,
1890   Ne drinke of herbes may ben his helpinge.
The vertu expulsif, or animal,
Fro thilke vertu cleped natural
Ne may the venym voiden ne expelle.
The pipes of his longes gonne to swelle,
And every lacerte in his brest adoun
Is shent with venym and corrupcioun.
Him gaineth neither, for to gete his lif,
Vomit upward, ne dounward laxatif.
Al is tobrosten thilke regioun;
1900   Nature hath now no dominacioun.
And certeinly, ther Nature wol nat wirche,
Fare wel phisik! go ber the man to chirche!
This al and som, that Arcita moot die;
For which he sendeth after Emelye,
And Palamon, that was his cosin deere.
Thanne seyde he thus, as ye shal after heere:
'Naught may the woful spirit in myn herte

Declare o point of alle my sorwes smerte
To yow, my lady, that I love moost;
But I biquethe the service of my goost   1910
To yow aboven every creature,
Sin that my lyf may no lenger dure.
Allas, the wo! allas, the peynes stronge,
That I for yow have suffred, and so longe!
Allas, the deeth! allas, myn Emelye!
Allas, departinge of oure compaignye!
Allas, myn hertes queene! allas, my wyf!
Myn hertes lady, endere of my lyf!
What is this world? what asketh men to have?
Now with his love, now in his colde grave   1920
Allone, withouten any compaignye.
Fare wel, my sweete foo, myn Emelye!
And softe taak me in youre armes tweye,
For love of God, and herkneth what I seye.

   I have heer with my cosin Palamon
Had strif and rancour many a day agon
For love of yow, and for my jalousye.
And Juppiter so wis my soule gye,
To speken of a servaunt proprely,
With alle circumstances trewely—   1930
That is to seyen, trouthe, honour, knighthede,
Wisdom, humblesse, estaat, and heigh kinrede,
Fredom, and al that longeth to that art—
So Juppiter have of my soule part,
As in this world right now ne knowe I non
So worthy to ben loved as Palamon,
That serveth yow, and wol doon al his lyf.
And if that evere ye shul ben a wyf,
Foryet nat Palamon, the gentil man.'

1940
And with that word his speche faille gan,
For from his feet up to his brest was come
The coold of deeth, that hadde him overcome,
And yet mooreover for in his armes two
The vital strengthe is lost and al ago.
Oonly the intellect, withouten moore,
That dwelled in his herte syk and soore,
Gan faillen whan the herte felte deeth.
Dusked his eyen two and failled breeth,
But on his lady yet caste he his ye;

1950
His laste word was, 'Mercy, Emelye!'
His spirit chaunged hous and wente ther,
As I cam nevere, I kan nat tellen wher.
Therfore I stynte, I nam no divinistre;
Of soules finde I nat in this registre,
Ne me ne list thilke opinions to telle
Of hem, though that they writen wher they dwelle.
Arcite is coold, ther Mars his soule gye!
Now wol I speken forth of Emelye.

Shrighte Emelye and howleth Palamon,

1960
And Theseus his suster took anon
Swowninge, and baar hire fro the corps away.
What helpeth it to tarien forth the day
To tellen how she weep bothe eve and morwe?
For in swich cas wommen have swich sorwe,
Whan that hir housbondes ben from hem ago,
That for the moore part they sorwen so,
Or ellis fallen in swich maladye,
That at the laste certeinly they die.

Infinite been the sorwes and the teeres

1970
Of olde folk, and folk of tendre yeeres,
In al the toun for deeth of this Theban.

For him ther wepeth bothe child and man;
So greet weping was ther noon, certain,
Whan Ector was ybroght, al fressh yslain,
To Troye. Allas, the pitee that was ther,
Cracchinge of chekes, rentinge eek of heer.
'Why woldestow be deed,' thise wommen crye,
'And haddest gold ynough, and Emelye?'
No man mighte gladen Theseus,
Savinge his olde fader Egeus,   1980
That knew this worldes transmutacioun,
As he hadde seyn it chaunge bothe up and doun,
Joye after wo, and wo after gladnesse,
And shewed hem ensamples and liknesse.

  'Right as ther died nevere man,' quod he,
'That he ne livede in erthe in some degree,
Right so ther livede never man,' he seyde,
'In al this world, that som time he ne deyde.
This world nis but a thurghfare ful of wo,
And we been pilgrimes, passinge to and fro.   1990
Deeth is an ende of every worldly soore.'
And over al this yet seyde he muchel moore
To this effect, ful wisely to enhorte
The peple that they sholde hem reconforte.
Duc Theseus, with al his bisy cure,
Caste now wher that the sepulture
Of goode Arcite may best ymaked be,
And eek moost honurable in his degree.
And at the laste he took conclusioun
That ther as first Arcite and Palamoun   2000
Hadden for love the bataille hem bitwene,
That in that selve grove swoote and grene,
Ther as he hadde his amorouse desires,

His compleynte, and for love his hoote fires,
He wolde make a fyr in which the office
Funeral he mighte al accomplice.
And leet comande anon to hakke and hewe
The okes olde, and leye hem on a rewe
In colpons wel arrayed for to brenne.
His officers with swifte feet they renne
And ride anon at his comandement.
And after this, Theseus hath ysent
After a beere, and it al over spradde
With clooth of gold, the richeste that he hadde.
And of the same suite he cladde Arcite;
Upon his hondes hadde he gloves white,
Eek on his heed a coroune of laurer grene,
And in his hond a swerd ful bright and kene.
He leyde him, bare the visage, on the beere;
Therwith he weep that pitee was to heere.
And for the peple sholde seen him alle,
Whan it was day he broghte him to the halle,
That roreth of the crying and the soun.

Tho cam this woful Theban Palamoun,
With flotery berd and ruggy, asshy heeres,
In clothes blake, ydropped al with teeres;
And, passinge othere of wepinge, Emelye,
The rewefulleste of al the compaignye.
In as muche as the service sholde be
The moore noble and riche in his degree,
Duc Theseus leet forth thre steedes bringe,
That trapped were in steel al gliteringe,
And covered with the armes of daun Arcite.
Upon thise steedes, that weren grete and white,
Ther seten folk, of whiche oon baar his sheeld,

2010

2020

2030

146

Another his spere up on his hondes heeld,
The thridde baar with him his bowe Turkeys
(Of brend gold was the caas and eek the harneys);
And riden forth a paas with sorweful cheere
Toward the grove, as ye shul after heere.   2040
The nobleste of the Grekes that ther were
Upon hir shuldres carieden the beere,
With slakke paas, and eyen rede and wete,
Thurghout the citee by the maister strete,
That sprad was al with blak, and wonder hye
Right of the same is the strete ywrye.
Upon the right hond wente olde Egeus,
And on that oother side duc Theseus,
With vessels in hir hand of gold ful fyn,
Al ful of hony, milk, and blood, and wyn;   2050
Eek Palamon, with ful greet compaignye;
And after that cam woful Emelye,
With fyr in honde, as was that time the gyse,
To do the office of funeral servise.

   Heigh labour and ful greet apparaillinge
Was at the service and the fyr-makinge,
That with his grene top the hevene raughte;
And twenty fadme of brede the armes straughte—
This is to seyn, the bowes weren so brode.
Of stree first ther was leyd ful many a lode.   2060
But how the fyr was maked upon highte,
Ne eek the names that the trees highte,
As ook, firre, birch, aspe, alder, holm, popler,
Wilugh, elm, plane, assh, box, chasteyn, linde, laurer,
Mapul, thorn, bech, hasel, ew, whippeltree—
How they weren feld, shal nat be toold for me;
Ne hou the goddes ronnen up and doun,

Disherited of hire habitacioun,
In which they woneden in reste and pees,
2070   Nymphes, fawnes and amadrides;
Ne hou the beestes and the briddes alle
Fledden for fere, whan the wode was falle;
Ne how the ground agast was of the light,
That was nat wont to seen the sonne bright;
Ne how the fyr was couched first with stree,
And thanne with drye stikkes cloven a thre,
And thanne with grene wode and spicerye,
And thanne with clooth of gold and with perrye,
And gerlandes, hanginge with ful many a flour;
2080   The mirre, th'encens, with al so greet odour;
Ne how Arcite lay among al this,
Ne what richesse aboute his body is;
Ne how that Emelye, as was the gyse,
Putte in the fyr of funeral servise;
Ne how she swowned whan men made the fyr,
Ne what she spak, ne what was hir desir;
Ne what jeweles men in the fire caste,
Whan that the fyr was greet and brente faste;
Ne how somme caste hir sheeld, and somme hir spere,
2090   And of hire vestimentz, whiche that they were,
And coppes fulle of wyn, and milk, and blood,
Into the fyr, that brente as it were wood;
Ne how the Grekes, with an huge route,
Thries riden al the fyr aboute
Upon the left hand, with a loud shoutinge,
And thries with hir speres clateringe;
And thries how the ladies gonne crye;
Ne how that lad was homward Emelye;
Ne how Arcite is brent to asshen colde;

Ne how that lyche-wake was yholde   2100
Al thilke night; ne how the Grekes pleye
The wake-pleyes, ne kepe I nat to seye;
Who wrastleth best naked with oille enoint,
Ne who that baar him best, in no disjoint.
I wol nat tellen eek how that they goon
Hoom til Atthenes, whan the pley is doon;
But shortly to the point thanne wol I wende,
And maken of my longe tale an ende.

By processe and by lengthe of certeyn yeres,
Al stynted is the moorninge and the teres   2110
Of Grekes, by oon general assent.
Thanne semed me ther was a parlement
At Atthenes upon certein pointz and caas;
Among the whiche pointz yspoken was
To have with certein contrees alliaunce,
And have fully of Thebans obeisaunce.
For which this noble Theseus anon
Leet senden after gentil Palamon,
Unwist of him what was the cause and why;
But in his blake clothes sorwefully   2120
He cam at his comandement in hye.
Tho sente Theseus for Emelye.
Whan they were set, and hust was al the place,
And Theseus abiden hadde a space
Er any word cam fram his wise brest,
His eyen sette he ther as was his lest.
And with a sad visage he siked stille,
And after that right thus he seyde his wille:

'The Firste Moevere of the cause above,
Whan he first made the faire cheyne of love,   2130
Greet was th'effect, and heigh was his entente.

Wel wiste he why, and what thereof he mente;
For with that faire cheyne of love he bond
The fyr, the eyr, the water, and the lond
In certeyn boundes, that they may nat flee.
That same Prince and that Moevere,' quod he,
'Hath stablissed in this wrecched world adoun
Certeyne dayes and duracioun
To al that is engendred in this place,
2140   Over the whiche day they may nat pace,
Al mowe they yet tho dayes wel abregge.
Ther nedeth noght noon auctoritee t'allegge,
For it is preeved by experience,
But that me list declaren my sentence.
Thanne may men by this ordre wel discerne
That thilke Moevere stable is and eterne.
Wel may men knowe, but it be a fool,
That every part dirriveth from his hool;
For nature hath nat taken his biginning
2150   Of no partie or cantel of a thing,
But of a thing that parfit is and stable,
Descendinge so til it be corrumpable.
And therfore, of his wise purveiaunce,
He hath so wel biset his ordinaunce
That speces of thinges and progressiouns
Shullen enduren by successiouns,
And nat eterne, withouten any lie.
This maystow understonde and seen at ye.
    Loo the ook, that hath so long a norisshinge
2160   From time that it first biginneth to springe,
And hath so long a lif, as we may see,
Yet at the laste wasted is the tree.
Considereth eek how that the harde stoon

Under oure feet, on which we trede and goon,
Yet wasteth it as it lyth by the weye.
The brode river somtime wexeth dreye;
The grete tounes se we wane and wende.
Thanne may ye se that al this thing hath ende.

Of man and womman seen we wel also
That nedes, in oon of thise termes two, 2170
This is to seyn, in youthe or elles age,
He moot be deed, the king as shal a page;
Som in his bed, som in the depe see,
Som in the large feeld, as men may see;
Ther helpeth noght, al goth that ilke weye.
Thanne may I seyn that al this thing moot deye.

What maketh this but Juppiter, the king,
That is prince and cause of alle thing,
Convertinge al unto his propre welle
From which it is dirrived, sooth to telle? 2180
And heer-agains no creature on live,
Of no degree, availleth for to strive.

Thanne is it wisdom, as it thinketh me,
To maken vertu of necessitee,
And take it weel that we may nat eschue,
And namely that to us alle is due.
And whoso gruccheth ought, he dooth folye,
And rebel is to him that al may gye.
And certeinly a man hath moost honour
To dien in his excellence and flour, 2190
Whan he is siker of his goode name;
Thanne hath he doon his freend ne him no shame.
And gladder oghte his freend been of his deeth,
Whan with honour up yolden is his breeth,
Than whan his name apalled is for age,

For al forgeten is his vassellage.
Thanne is it best, as for a worthy fame,
To dien whan that he is best of name.
    The contrarie of al this is wilfulnesse.
2200 Why grucchen we, why have we hevinesse,
That goode Arcite, of chivalrie the flour,
Departed is with duetee and honour
Out of this foule prisoun of this lyf?
Why grucchen heere his cosin and his wyf
Of his welfare, that loved hem so weel?
Kan he hem thank? Nay, God woot, never a deel,
That both his soule and eek hemself offende,
And yet they mowe hir lustes nat amende.
    What may I conclude of this longe serye,
2210 But after wo I rede us to be merye,
And thanken Juppiter of al his grace?
And er that we departen from this place
I rede that we make of sorwes two
O parfit joye, lastinge everemo.
And looketh now, wher moost sorwe is herinne,
Ther wol we first amenden and biginne.
    Suster,' quod he, 'this is my fulle assent,
With al th'avis heere of my parlement,
That gentil Palamon, youre owene knight,
2220 That serveth yow with wille, herte, and might,
And ever hath doon sin ye first him knewe,
That ye shul of youre grace upon him rewe,
And taken him for housbonde and for lord.
Lene me youre hond, for this is oure accord.
Lat se now of youre wommanly pitee.
He is a kinges brother sone, pardee;
And though he were a povre bacheler,

Sin he hath served yow so many a yeer,
And had for yow so greet adversitee,
It moste been considered, leeveth me;   2230
For gentil mercy oghte to passen right.'
   Thanne seyde he thus to Palamon the knight:
'I trowe ther nedeth litel sermoning
To make yow assente to this thing.
   Com neer, and taak youre lady by the hond.'
Bitwixen hem was maad anon the bond
That highte matrimoigne or mariage,
By al the conseil and the baronage.
And thus with alle blisse and melodye
Hath Palamon ywedded Emelye.   2240
And God, that al this wide world hath wroght,
Sende him his love that hath it deere aboght;
For now is Palamon in alle wele,
Livinge in blisse, in richesse, and in heele,
And Emelye him loveth so tendrely,
And he hire serveth al so gentilly,
That nevere was ther no word hem bitwene
Of jalousie or any oother teene.
Thus endeth Palamon and Emelye;
And God save al this faire compaignye! Amen.   2250

NOTES

1. *olde stories* It is characteristic of medieval writers to take pride not in their originality but in the authority conferred by ancient sources. Sometimes indeed they refer to sources which we may suspect never existed. In this case Chaucer's main source is the *Teseida* of Boccaccio, but since Boccaccio was a contemporary it cannot fairly be described as 'old'. Chaucer may possibly have wished his audience to think that his source was classical Latin, not modern Italian—Statius rather than Boccaccio—just as in *Troilus and Criseyde*, also translated from Boccaccio, he speaks of his authority as being a Latin author called Lollius (who never existed).

2. *duc* Like other medieval authors, Chaucer 'medievalized' the past, and gave great men titles of nobility current in his own time. There was a 'Duke of Athens' in the fourteenth century.

7. *What with* 'by means of'.

8. *regne of Femenye* 'realm of the Amazons'. *Femenye* is a name invented in the Middle Ages (from Latin *femina*, 'woman') for the mythical country of Amazonia, inhabited entirely by women.

12. *solempnitee* 'ceremony' or 'festivity'. In Middle English this word did not possess its modern suggestions of seriousness.

15. 'I leave this noble ruler riding to Athens.' We must expect in medieval narrative, which was normally meant for listeners, not readers with their own copies of the text, a certain 'openness' in the manipulation of the story-material. The author will tell us when he is going to take up a particular subject, and again when he is going to leave it: for an audience of listeners, all such transitions must be made unmistakably clear. In this case, the Knight is about to embark on a brief digression explaining why he does *not* intend to deal with certain material; and at the end of it, in lines 34–5, he returns to his story with an even more emphatic transition.

17–27. An example of the rhetorical figure called *occupatio*, by which a writer explains what he is *not* going to say. The figure may be used as a means of surreptitiously mentioning something while pretending not to mention it; but here it is a quite genuine indication of an omission of source-material, since the events summarized by Chaucer in twenty lines are narrated at length in over a thousand lines in the *Teseida*.

18–19. *manere How* 'way in which'.

20. *chivalrye* This word may either mean the accomplishments of a particular knight (as in line 7 above) or a company of knights (as probably here). It is sometimes not clear which sense is intended, *chivalrye* being a word of strong emotional associations but rather imprecise content.

21. *for the nones* 'particularly'. The phrase is one of the many almost meaningless tags available in the idiom of Middle English poetry as rhymes or fillers of metrical space. Here clearly the phrase is used for the rhyme with *Amazones*. Such tags are natural in the style of a poetry intended for reading aloud, since they give the audience time to catch up with the narrative.

22. *Atthenes* (here) 'Athenians'.

27. *as* This word is often used by Chaucer redundantly in adverbial phrases.

27–8. This metaphor, of ploughing for writing, is not uncommon in medieval literature. It is worth remembering that agricultural imagery, which might seem affected in the mouth of a modern soldier, would be much more familiar to medieval people, living in a society of small towns based on agriculture.

31. 'Also I do not wish to hinder any of this company.'

33. *lat se now* 'then let us see'.

31–3. The pilgrims had agreed before setting out that they would tell tales in turn to pass away the time on the journey to and from Canterbury, and that the one who was considered to have told the best tale would be given a supper by the whole company when they returned to the Tabard Inn.

39. *that* Often used redundantly in relative constructions in Middle English.

40. *tweye and tweye* 'two by two'—a first indication of the symmetrical order which is characteristic of the poem's action.

41. *Ech after oother* 'one behind another'.

42–4. It is typical of medieval poetry, and particularly of romances, to present a fictional world in which everything is superlative—the best or the worst, the richest, the loudest, the sweetest of its kind. The extreme thus becomes a quality of the invented world itself rather than of any particular incident within it.

55–6. The swoon was added by Chaucer. Pathos is a favourite effect of his, and of later medieval literature in general. Pity (*routhe* in line 56, *pitee* in line 62) was an emotion valued very highly then; in literature, at least, we tend to be more suspicious of it. But, as the last note above indicates, the extreme is a pervasive quality of medieval literary expression, and particularly perhaps the expression of emotions.

57–8. The first of many indications that the world of the poem, like the world as seen by Boethius (see p. 53 above), is governed by Fortune, the fickle goddess. The lady seems to hint that even Theseus's seemingly complete triumph is unstable; and Theseus is the one stable point in the poem.

65. *That she ne hath* 'who has not'.

66. *as it is wel seene* 'as is perfectly clear'.

67. *Thanked be* 'thanks to'. Fortune was regularly pictured with a moving wheel, which raised people to prosperity and dropped them to misery.

68. 'Who (i.e. Fortune) gives secure prosperity to no condition of life.' This reference to the universality of Fortune's fickleness again seems to glance at Theseus himself: as the ladies used to be, so he is; as they are, so he may be.

70. *Clemence* Like Fortune, a deified abstraction such as actually became part of Roman religion (Clementia's temple is mentioned by Statius), and was passed on as a way of thinking to the Middle Ages.

74. *Cappaneus* One of the seven who besieged Thebes, Theseus being another of them.

84. 'To do dishonour to the corpses.'

89. A horrifyingly blunt and concrete picture as the climax to a brilliant speech. Particularly from line 73 onwards, the lady's statement is admirably constructed, supplying all the necessary information to explain their situation to Theseus and organizing it into a complex syntactical structure, yet at the same time conveying a gradually intensifying emotion. This emerges in the interjections ('wrecche...cursed be that day!...weylaway') and through accusations that invoke explicit moral judgements ('Fulfild of ire and of iniquitee... for despit and for his tirannye'). With seeming naturalness, these parentheses interrupt the flow of sense, but they never completely break its continuity. The emotion culminates in the emphatic fourfold negative of lines 87–8. The final disclosure of what is involved in Creon's *iniquitee* and *tirannye*—

dogs eating human bodies. The speech, though unostenta-
tious, is a masterpiece of Chaucerian rhetoric.

97–8. 'When he saw those who had formerly been of such high
rank now so pitiful and so downcast.'

102–3. 'He would do everything in his power to avenge them
on the tyrant Creon.'

105–6. It is particularly noticeable at this early point how close
vindictiveness lies below the surface of pity.

of Theseus yserved As he that 'treated by Theseus like someone who'.

109. *To Thebes-ward* 'towards Thebes'.

110. *go ne ride* 'walk or ride', a tag used simply for emphasis,
and not to be taken literally.

112. 'But he camped that night on his journey towards Thebes.'

117–22. These details are added by Chaucer. He evokes the
pageantry of medieval warfare, and at the same time, in the
reference to Mars, hints at the sinister supernatural forces at
work behind the human action.

119. 'That the fields all about glittered with its brilliance.'

122. The Minotaur was a monster, half bull and half man,
which lived in Crete and devoured Athenian boys and girls
sent to it as tribute, until Theseus killed it. For further
comment, see Introduction, p. 68.

126. *Faire* 'satisfactorily, as planned'. A term of praise with
little precise meaning, but helping to provide the alliteration
that tends to accompany battles in this poem.

127–42. *But shortly for to speken of this thing…But it were al to
longe for to devyse…But shortly for to telle is myn entente* Expressions of a wish to be brief are common in medieval narrative
poetry, though sometimes as substitutes for brevity itself, to
give the impression that the poet is trying to speed things up.
They belong to a literature intended for audiences of listeners,
who might get bored, and whose presence must be recognized.
In *The Knight's Tale*, however, they are usually signs that
Chaucer really is abbreviating his sources.

135. 'To carry out funeral ceremonies according to the custom
of the time.' Though nearly all the detail of the action is
medieval, Chaucer reminds us every so often that it took place
in the past, and that customs then were different from what
they are in his own time. In this case, the bodies were burnt,
whereas the medieval practice was burial.

136. 'But it would take very much too long to describe.'

146. The lack of explicitness sounds sinister: another hint of the savagery involved in Theseus's chivalrous response to the ladies' request.

149. 'The pillagers worked with diligence and care.' They were working perhaps partly officially and partly on their own account.

153-4. Amidst the confusion of the battlefield the two knights are arranged as symmetrically as the company of ladies. Symmetry will be a persistent quality in their story.

154. *in oon armes* 'in the same armour'.

158-61. Over their armour, medieval knights wore jackets (*cote-armures*) bearing their heraldic devices. The heralds would be able to identify them by these, and thus would be able to tell that they were of noble family and might therefore bring in a ransom if captured.

159-60. *knewe hem best in special As they that weren* 'recognized them distinctly as being'.

166. *he nolde no raunsoun* 'he would not accept any ransom'. It is not clear whether Theseus is acting nobly in refusing to sell prisoners for money or cruelly (in which case *worthy* in the next line must be taken ironically) in condemning them to perpetual imprisonment. In either case, his decisive power is enacted in the brevity and directness of lines which offer no explanation.

171. *Terme of his lyf* 'for the duration of his life'.

    what nedeth wordes mo? A casual remark, little more than a tag; but its very casualness has a meaning. Already we are being conditioned to expect a world in which, as a matter of course, opposite extremes of the human condition will co-exist—Theseus 'in joye and in honour' for ever, the two knights 'in angwissh and in wo' for ever—with no comment either necessary or possible.

177-81. The effect of the three comparisons—with the lily, the rose, and May itself—is to make Emelye almost a personification of the season, rather than a person in her own right. Belonging to a long convention in medieval poetry, this May morning setting has become almost symbolic by Chaucer's time: the youth and beauty of the lady and the freshness of the season have become the expression of feelings rather than the objective description of facts. The references were added by Chaucer.

187. *Arys and do thyn observaunce* 'rise up and perform the

rites of May'. On May Day it was the custom to get up early in the morning, walk in the fields or woods, and make garlands of may-flowers. The recurrence of such seasonal rituals in medieval life is the cause and justification for seasonal conventions in medieval literature.

193. *at the sonne upriste* 'at sunrise'.

195. *party white and rede* May-blossom is mixed white and red in colour; on the other hand, the branches are prickly, and hence not very suitable for a garland to be worn.

198. *The grete tour* The part of a medieval castle that was used as a place of refuge, not the part that was lived in.

200-1. Another example of the 'open' manipulation of story-material referred to in the note on line 15 above.

202. *evene joinant* 'right next to'.

203. *hadde hir pleyinge* 'was amusing herself'.

215. 'He often said, "Alas that I was born".'

216. *by aventure or cas* 'by accident or chance'. The two are not really alternatives, but serve as an emphatic way of saying that what happened happened accidentally, not by anyone's choice—part of the contingency of a world governed by Fortune.

217-18. 'That through a window, thickly barred with pieces of iron as solid and strong as beams.'

224. *on to see* 'to look at'.

226-7. 'For the love of God, endure our prison with complete patience, for it cannot be altered.' Here Arcite produces spontaneously the same philosophy of despairing endurance that emerges from Theseus's reflexions at the end of the poem: 'take it weel that we may nat eschue' (2185).

228-33. Here once again Fortune is referred to, and, to judge from the abrupt transition, is identified by Arcite with the influence of the planetary deities.

229-30. *aspect...disposicioun...constellacioun* In astrology, the *aspect* of planets was their position relative to one another and to the earth, their *disposicioun* was simply their position, and their *constellacioun* was their position at the time when someone was born, which might influence his whole life. Arcite seems to be using the words rather vaguely, much as a modern person might loosely employ technical psycho-analytic terms ('complex', 'neurosis', etc.). Saturn was normally a planet of evil influence, as he himself explains later; see lines 1595–611.

231. *although we hadde it sworn* 'although we had sworn to the contrary', cf. lines 808–9.

233. *this is the short and plain* 'that is the long and short of it'.

235–6. *of this opinioun Thow hast a veyn imaginacioun* 'this belief of yours is an empty fantasy'.

239. *that wol my bane be* 'and it will be the death of me'. Arcite had supposed that Palamon was crying out in misery at the thought of their imprisonment; in fact, his 'wound' was caused by love.

243–4. In Virgil's *Aeneid*, Aeneas, meeting a beautiful maiden, had asked whether she was a mortal or a goddess; it was in fact Venus in disguise. Here the idea is taken up again, though Emelye is *not* Venus; and this explains the use of the word *transfigure* in line 247.

246–53. This reverent attitude of Palamon's towards Venus is in keeping with his later prayer to Venus (lines 1363–402). The present speech was added by Chaucer; in Boccaccio it is Arcite who sees Emelye first.

250–1. 'And if it should be that it is my fate, fixed by an eternal decree, to die in prison.'

252. *oure linage* i.e. the royal house of Thebes.

262. *hir mercy and hir grace* Like the idea of wounds and death being caused by love, these terms belong to the esoteric language of medieval courtly love. The beloved lady is thought of as a goddess (cf. lines 243–4 above), and any reciprocal feelings she may have are a matter of mercy on her part, not of desert on her lover's.

263. 'So that I may at least see her.'

264. *I nam but deed* 'it will simply be the death of me'.

269. 'May God help me, I feel very little like joking.'

271–82. The structure of this long sentence is rather confused, though it would be clear enough in practice when read aloud. There is a kind of stammer in the syntax which expresses Palamon's incoherence under the pressure of emotion.

273–4. *thy brother Ysworn ful depe* They are 'sworn brothers', that is, they have taken an oath to regard each other as brothers, a situation frequently mentioned in medieval literature.

275. *for to dyen in the peyne* 'though we were to die by torture'.

285. In Palamon's calling Emelye, of whom he has had only a glimpse, 'my lady', and in the disputation that follows about their right to a woman who knows nothing of their existence, there is clearly an extravagance that touches on absurdity. The absurdity is indeed hinted at in the curt dismissal of

lines 329–31; it is perhaps seen by Chaucer but not by the Knight.

286. *til that myn herte sterve* 'till my heart ceases to beat'.

288–9. *tolde thee my wo As to my conseil* 'discussed my misery with you as with someone in my confidence'.

293. *I dar wel seyn* 'I can confidently say'.

295–301. '"It is more likely", he said, "that you are false than that I am; and indeed I tell you outright that you *are* false. For I loved her first, before you did, as a man loves a woman. What will you answer to that? You don't know even now whether she is a woman or a goddess. Your feeling is one of religious devotion, and mine is one of human love".' A clever piece of quibbling on Arcite's part, though some scholars have seen it as indicating a fundamental difference of character between Palamon and Arcite.

305. The *olde clerk* is Boethius, in the *De Consolatione Philosophiae*, where the *sawe* is applied to Orpheus and Eurydice.

306–11. The interlocking repetitions 'lovere...lawe...love... lawe...lawe...love...love' emphasize the two concepts played against each other in Arcite's argument.

309. *positif lawe and swich decree* 'human (as opposed to natural) law and all such mere enactments'.

312. *sholde be deed* 'were to die'.

313. *Al be she* 'whether the woman he loves is'.

314–15. *it is nat...hir grace* 'you are not likely at any time in your life to receive her favour'.

318. *us gaineth no raunsoun* 'no ransom will help us'.

319–22. A variant of a fable in Aesop, in which a fox runs off with a titbit while a lion and a tiger are quarrelling over it.

320. *hir part was noon* 'neither got a share of it'.

324. 'Every man for himself, that's all there is for it.' The saying was evidently proverbial.

339. 'And Theseus loved Pirithous as tenderly in return.'

340. *as olde bookes sayn* Vague references of this kind to ancient written authorities are common in medieval literature. In this case the 'old book' is probably the *Roman de la Rose*, where the story is told in the form given here. In classical literature the story is that Pirithous accompanied Theseus to hell to carry off Proserpina.

343. The story is supposed to be told aloud by the Knight, not written. This line may conceivably derive from the earlier form of the Tale as *Palamon and Arcite*, or, more likely, it

may simply reflect the fact that at this point Chaucer had forgotten to distinguish between himself and the Knight as storytellers. Compare *endite* in line 351 below.

352. *him Arcite* 'this Arcite'. A common Middle English idiom.

353. *if so were* 'if it should happen'.

359. *taketh* 'he (Arcite) takes'.

363. A characteristic Chaucerian formula for extreme grief. Compare the notes on lines 42–4 and 55–6 above.

364. 'He looks out for a chance to commit suicide secretly.' In Chaucer, the intention to commit suicide tends to be little more than another formula for intense grief; it is rarely put into practice. In *The Franklin's Tale* the heroine, after listing twenty-one examples of ladies who have killed themselves rather than be dishonoured, does *not* kill herself.

366. Arcite is released from a physical prison into a metaphysical prison that is no less real; the prison becomes an image for human life itself.

367. *is me shape* 'I am destined'.

368. *purgatorie...helle* According to medieval Catholic theology, souls in purgatory were being punished for a finite time before being allowed into heaven, while those in hell were punished eternally. Throughout this speech, Arcite implies a 'theology' of secular love which parodies Christian theology: note also *eternally* (line 367), *blisse* (line 372), *grace* (line 374), and the idea in lines 373–5 that the mere sight of Emelye would have been reward enough for him, just as the chief reward of the blessed souls is the sight of God. Similarly, the chief punishment of the damned is being deprived of the sight of God, just as Arcite is deprived of the sight of Emelye.

378–9. *blisfully...paradys* The theological language is continued.

380–1. 'Fortune has cast the dice well for you, who are in sight of her, while I am absent from her.' Chaucer often uses gambling imagery to express the unpredictability of Fortune.

387. *dispeir* Another theological term (identical in meaning with *wanhope* in line 391 below), meaning despair of God's mercy, the ultimate sin, which makes salvation impossible.

388–9. According to medieval physics, all created substances were made from the four elements of earth, water, fire, and air.

393–409. These lines, dealing philosophically with man's ignorance of what he wishes for in life, are based on Boethius. For comment on them, see Introduction, pp. 72–3.

Notes

393–4. 'Alas, why do people so commonly complain about the providence of God or of Fortune.'

397–9. *Som...som* 'one...another'.

399. 'And another man would willingly leave his prison.'

403–6. The image of the drunkard is all the more effective for being more familiar and immediate than we should expect in philosophical discourse; it comes from Boethius, typically Chaucerian though it sounds.

416. *I nam but deed* 'I am as good as dead'.

431. *to lady and to wyf* 'as your lady and as your wife'. Lady implies a courtly love relationship.

436. *that sterve here in a cage* 'who am dying here behind bars'.

443. *he lyk was to biholde* 'to look at he was like'.

444. *boxtree* The wood of this tree is very pale, and is traditionally used as an image for human pallor both in English and in Latin.

445–75. For comment on this speech, see Introduction, pp. 74–5.

447. *table of atthamaunt* The decrees of the gods being eternal, they are appropriately thought of as being inscribed on a tablet made from adamant, an indestructible stone.

449. 'Why is mankind under any greater obligation to you.'

455–6. 'What order is there in this foreknowledge by which the innocent are causelessly tormented?' Chaucer returns again and again in his poetry to the problems raised by the hypothesis of divine foreknowledge: does it deprive man of his freewill, and, where the foreknowledge of disasters is concerned, does it imply callousness in God (or the gods)? Such problems were discussed by Boethius, but they were still living issues in the Christian philosophy of Chaucer's own time.

457–60. 'And my suffering is increased still further by the thought that man is bound by his duty to God to refrain from doing what he wishes, whereas a beast may fulfil all its desires.'

460–1. *his...he* We should use 'its' and 'it'.

463. *have* Subjunctive: 'may have had'.

464. *it may stonden so* 'that may be how things happen'.

465–6. 'I leave the solution of this problem to theologians, but I know well that there is great suffering in this world.' The contrast between the theory of the authorities and the knowledge that one derives from one's own experience is a common one in Chaucer.

163

467–9. 'Alas, one can see serpents or thieves, who have done harm to many good men, going about at liberty and wandering where they choose.'

470–1. Arcite has earlier (line 230) suggested that Saturn is to blame for the imprisonment of the two knights; here the planet Saturn merges into the pagan god, in a way which is typical of medieval poetry with a pagan setting, but which makes it difficult to know how far the astrology is to be interpreted 'theologically'. The anger of the goddess Juno (not a planet) is mentioned by both Statius and Boccaccio as the cause for the destruction of Thebes and the persecution of the Thebans.

474. Venus is a planetary goddess, but is here also used to refer to the human motive for which she was supposed to be responsible—sexual love.

475. *him Arcite* We might colloquially say 'that Arcite'.

476–8. Another example of the kind of 'open' transition mentioned in the note on line 15.

482. *mester* 'occupation'. Chaucer is writing as though 'lover' and 'prisoner' were trades or professions.

486. *upon his heed* 'on pain of death'.

487. *as out of that contree* The *as* is probably redundant, as is often the case at the beginning of adverbial phrases in Middle English. But it may imply a kind of apology for speaking of Arcite as being 'exiled' from a country where he had dwelt only as a prisoner, in which case one could translate 'so far as that country was concerned'.

489–94. Medieval courtly poetry often leads up to an explicit question, often concerning love, a *demande d'amour*, which is to be answered not by the poet but by his audience. In the courts of the Middle Ages, poetry was a communal form of entertainment: a poem would be more effective as a pastime if it offered matter for discussion by its audience.

493. *wher him list* 'wherever he pleases'.

497–521. Extreme grief is here presented in terms of the conventional psychological and physical symptoms; note particularly the superlative convention (referred to in the note on lines 42–4) offered in lines 500–2 as a summary of Arcite's condition.

503. 'He lost his ability to sleep, eat, and drink.'

511–18. In the Middle Ages, psychology was very closely related to a traditional (though completely unscientific) physiology. This fact is particularly relevant to the interpretation of line 511: for us, to say of someone that his spirits are low is to speak metaphorically; in the Middle Ages, the statement had a literal sense. Human life was supposed to be dependent on three 'virtues' or 'spirits', which were conceived of as fluids carried about the body by the blood. The 'loveris maladye of Hereos' (derived from the Greek word *eros*, meaning 'love') was thought of as an actual disease from which lovers suffered, with the symptoms described in this passage. If it was not cured, according to some authorities, it led to mania (the *manie* of line 516). The brain was divided into three cells, the front one concerned with 'phantasy' (i.e. perception), the middle one with reason, the back one with memory. Mania was thought of as a disease of the *celle fantastik*, caused by an excess of the humour of melancholy, one of the four liquids which governed the whole condition of the body.

512. *chaunged so* 'he was so changed'.

518. 'At the front of his head, in the cell of perception.'

520. *habit* Lovers are traditionally careless in their dress.

521. *daun* A title of respect, which can variously be translated 'lord', 'master', 'sir', etc.

527–34. This vision of Mercury was added to Boccaccio by Chaucer, who generally makes the gods influence the human actions of the story more directly. Mercury, another planetary deity, was the messenger of the gods in classical mythology, the god of sleep and dreams, and also the god with whom oracles were particularly associated. He was generally described as wearing a winged cap (*hat*, line 530) and bearing a magic staff or 'caduceus' which was capable of sending people to sleep (*slepy yerde*, line 529). The incident of Argus is referred to by Ovid, from whom Chaucer may have taken his description: Argus was a monster with a hundred eyes who was set as a guard over Io by Juno, but was sent to sleep and then killed by Mercury.

534. An example of dramatic irony; for the end of Arcite's misery will indeed come in Athens, but only through his death. The irony is cruel, and this is in keeping with the way the gods are presented in this story.

536. *hou soore that me smerte* 'however much it hurts me'.

538–9. *Ne for . . . To se* 'And the fear of death will not cause me to give up seeing.'

540. 'I do not care if I die, so long as I am with her.' Another case of dramatic irony: he does eventually die in her presence.

554. *Which* 'who'.

560. *chamberleyn* The official of a large household who was in charge of the bed-chamber arrangements.

562–3. 'For he was prudent, and was soon able to discover which among the servants served her.'

565. *for the nones* See note on line 21.

567. 'Enough to do whatever anyone could order him.'

569–82. In being first *page of the chambre* to the duke's sister-in-law and then *squier* of the duke's chamber, Arcite is going through a normal course for any young man rising in the court world. Chaucer's own early career had followed a similar pattern.

574. 'That his reputation spread all through the court.'

575–6. *were a charitee That Theseus wolde* 'would be a kindness for Theseus to'.

580. *his goode tonge* The ability to speak well was highly valued in medieval courtly society, where one of the main social activities was conversation.

581–2. The ruler was the physical as well as the metaphorical centre of the medieval court, and Arcite, becoming intimate in friendship with Theseus, is given a position which brings him close to his person.

586. *honestly and slyly* 'suitably and discreetly'.

596–8. This form of question, to which the answer ('no one') is obvious, is a means of emphasis recommended by the medieval *artes poeticae*.

601–3. Another rhetorical question, to which an answer is immediately supplied. Here the effect intended is not entirely certain. To a modern reader, the lines sound somewhat deflating, as though Chaucer, if not the Knight, were less impressed than he might be by Palamon's misery. But the assertion of modesty (*diminutio*) and the promise to be brief are both familiar devices of the *artes poeticae*. Moreover, the idea of love as a martyrdom is a common one in medieval courtly literature, so that there is no need to read it as ironic.

604–5. We do not know of any source from which Chaucer could have got the date 3 May, and so the reference to *olde bookes* is presumably only a convention. It thus seems likely that the date was invented by Chaucer, and this has led some scholars to find a special significance in it, particularly since

it is a date he mentions elsewhere in his poetry. There is some
evidence to suggest that in medieval times it was considered
an unlucky day, but its exact significance, if any, is uncertain.

609. After a series of parentheses, Chaucer resumes the construc-
tion begun in line 604 by repeating the *that* of that line.

614. *opie of Thebes* This may be not the Thebes in Greece from
which the two knights come but another Thebes in Egypt,
which was famous for its opium. But Chaucer very likely
did not distinguish between the two. In the *Teseida* Palamon
was helped to escape by a Theban doctor. Chaucer makes the
whole episode of the escape less complicated, and thus the
repeated *fleeth...faste* of lines 611 and 617 becomes more
convincing and dramatic.

621. A most effective line, in conveying stealthy haste by trans-
ferring Palamon's dread to his feet, which are seen as it were
in close-up, stalking (with its associations with hunting)
through the grove. The whole narrative becomes more
exciting at this point, as Palamon begins to act decisively.

633–8. This description of early morning is in part conventional
and in part derived from particular sources (line 636, for
example, is translated from Dante). But it is not so conventional as it is likely to seem to a modern reader, for the
passage itself must have played an important part in establish-
ing the convention to which it now seems to belong. *The
Knight's Tale* was one of the works of Chaucer which retained
currency, at least among poets, right down to the seventeenth
century, and this passage certainly lies behind similar descriptions of early morning in Spenser, Shakespeare and Milton.
It is a fine passage, liquid in sound with its repeated l's and
r's, yet full of a living, reciprocal activity, in which the lark
greets the dawn, the east laughs with the light of the sun, and
the sun's rays dry the dew on the trees.

640. *squier principal* He has evidently been further promoted
in the interim.

642–54. A second May-time scene, paralleling the one of seven
years before, and also added by Chaucer.

646. *were it* 'perhaps'.

654. Part of the courtly game of love in the Middle Ages was a
division of the participants into two orders, those devoted to
the flower and those devoted to the leaf; and it may be that
Arcite's reference to *grene* alludes to this division, for we have
just been told that his garland is of leaves, not flowers. But

he may simply mean that he hopes to receive a garland from his beloved, or even in a vaguer sense, that he hopes for some possibility of growth, some favourable change in his situation.

658. *by aventure* The phrase has already been used in line 648 of Arcite's happening to come to this particular place. Throughout, Chaucer stresses the operation of chance, which is in effect the same as Fortune.

663–6. Chaucer is fond of such proverbial expansions of his material. They were recommended by the *artes poeticae*, which called them *sententiae*. The particular event is moralized and generalized, and thus made relevant to his audience's experience of life.

663. 'But for many years it has truly been said.'

665–6. 'It is a very good thing for a man to be on his guard, for people are always meeting unexpectedly.'

671. *roundel* A short poem with a refrain, originally sung to accompany a dance. Some lines from it are quoted above, lines 652–4.

673–81. These lines are clearly inessential to the development of the narrative, and it may be necessary for a modern reader to remind himself that the medieval conception of narrative was as a skeleton which needed to be clothed in the flesh of amplification. Diffuseness was a positive goal of certain types of medieval poetry; and indeed a diffuse style was probably more suitable for reading aloud to small audiences than the more concentrated styles of modern poetry. (Compare the style of Dickens's novels, which were also written to be read aloud.) And yet the actual content of this seeming digression is not irrelevant to the meaning of *The Knight's Tale*; for it asserts the power and unpredictability of one of the gods who control a story of which one of the points is its very randomness.

673. *thise loveres* Lovers in general.

674. A pleasantly rural way of saying 'in high spirits at one minute, in low spirits the next'. Chaucer lived in a predominantly agricultural society, where even the largest towns were small, and though he himself was a Londoner, his images constantly recall the countryside.

676–81. Friday was assigned to Venus (compare the Latin *veneris dies*, French *vendredi*), and it was a proverbial saying that Fridays were changeable, or at least, as line 681 suggests, that they tended to be different in weather from the rest of the week.

680. *array* Chaucer may be making use of the ambiguity of this word, which can mean either 'condition' in a general sense or, more specifically, 'dress'. Thus Venus's changefulness can be presented as the feminine trait of enjoying frequent changes of clothes.

684–713. These lines make up a formal lamentation (called *exclamatio* by the *artes poeticae*). They are not of course intended to sound natural, or to represent what a real person would actually have said on such an occasion, but to provide an expression of grief more noble and more moving than any 'spontaneous overflow of powerful feeling' could be. They are thus composed in a 'high style' which is clearly distinguishable from the surrounding verse by such characteristics as a Latinate vocabulary, syntax, and word-order, and a tendency to parallelisms like those found in the Psalms (e.g. 'Of his linage am I and his ofspring', 'so caytyf and so thral'). The speech is as formal, and as capable of moving us, as an operatic aria.

685–6. *Juno* See note on lines 470–1.

688. Cadmus was the founder of Thebes, and Amphion afterwards ruled it and built a wall round it.

708. 'My death was destined before my first clothes were made (i.e. before I was born).'

711–12. 'I don't care a jot for all my other sorrows.'

734. *by grace* A phrase belonging to a Christian context, and meaning 'by the grace of God', and hence, when used casually, 'by luck'. Here it must mean something like 'by fate': it falls into place as one of many references to the destiny, fortune, or blind chance that governs the poem's human actions.

745. *That thou ne sholdest dyen* 'without dying'.

754. *as a knight* 'equipped with knightly armour'.

761. *as for me* 'as far as I am concerned'.

764. *leyd his feith to borwe* 'pledged his honour (to keep the agreement)'.

765–9. Another *exclamatio*, followed by a *sententia* ('Ful sooth is seyd...'—compare the *sententia* beginning with 'But sooth is seyd...' in line 663), and then by a line explicitly linking the generalizing *sententia* with the particular situation.

765. 'O Cupid, lacking in all kindness.' Cupid is the son of Venus and god of love; he is the god of the courtly religion of love, and here his narrower kind of love, based on sexual

attraction, is contrasted with *charitee*, the natural love of the true religion.

766. 'O rule, that will permit no companion to share you.' This compressed line is expanded and explained by the couplet following.

767–8. 'It is said with great truth that neither sovereignty nor love will willingly accept any companionship.' That is to say, that the ruler insists on ruling alone and the lover on loving alone. The triple negative ('ne...noght...no') is used as a means of emphasis.

769. 'Arcite and Palamon certainly find that to be true.'

775. *allone as he was born* 'as alone as when he was born'.

780–8. An extended simile of the kind originally used by Homer and traditionally belonging to epic poetry. This one originates in Statius, is adapted for a different purpose by Boccaccio, and for a third purpose by Chaucer.

780. *hunters* Genitive singular.

784. *breketh* Professor Bennett points out in his edition of *The Knight's Tale* that though this word is syntactically parallel with *hereth* and *thinketh*, it would more naturally be used not of the hunter but of the animal as it crashes through the undergrowth. Thus, unusually in Chaucer, at this moment of excitement, the syntax takes on a Shakespearean ambiguity.

791–802. The way in which this incident is presented makes it a perfect example of how, in the world of *The Knight's Tale*, chivalric courtesy and humanity are the brave trappings of brutal violence. The touching brotherliness with which they arm each other is succeeded immediately by the images of savage animals describing their attack on each other. The whole scene is of course exaggerated, if judged by realistic standards; but the exaggeration serves not merely to excite but to make a serious point about the nature of the chivalric life.

792. *rehersing* 'repetition (of their agreement)'.

797–8. *mightest wene...were* 'might have supposed...was'.

803. *I lete hem fighting dwelle* Literally, 'I leave them remaining fighting', i.e. 'I leave them still fighting'.

805–14. This philosophical digression is based on Boccaccio but is stiffened with reminiscences of Boethius's more comprehensive philosophy, in which the pagan conception of Destiny is subordinated to the Christian conception of divine Providence, so that Destiny becomes the *ministre general* of Providence.

809. *by ye or nay* 'definitely'.

810–11. 'Yet sometimes an event will happen on a certain day that does not happen again in a thousand years.'

814. *sighte* 'Providence'.

815. *This mene I now by* 'I say this with reference to'.

817. *namely at the grete hert* 'especially (to hunt) the great hart'. A 'great hart' was thought of as especially noble game for the hunt.

818–19. *in his bed ther daweth him no day That he nis clad* A mixture of two different constructions. 'No dawn finds him still in bed, but he is dressed.'

824. Mars is the god of war, Diana the goddess of hunting. We are constantly reminded, even in such casual and apparently decorative ways, of the powers which rule the world of the poem.

833. *rideth him* 'rides'. *Him* is a redundant reflexive pronoun.

836. *cours* 'pursuit' or 'chase', a technical hunting term.

839. *Under the sonne* 'shading his eyes against the sun'.

841. *as it were bores two* 'like two wild boars'. The preceding picture of Theseus as a hunter redoubles the effect of the beast-imagery applied to Palamon and Arcite. Their brutality is underlined, and his role comes to seem that of a tamer of the savagery of men as well as wild animals.

853. *for to* 'as to'.

860. 'Whose lives are a burden to us.'

878. *it am I* The usual Middle English idiom for 'It is I'.

888. *pine yow with the corde* One medieval torture, used to force a suspect to confess, was to tie his wrists behind his back and haul him up and down by them. This is perhaps what Theseus is referring to.

889. *by mighty Mars the rede* The planet Mars is red in colour.

890–2. A. E. Housman, the poet and distinguished classical scholar, wrote of these lines, 'If Homer or Dante had the same thing to say, would he wish to say it otherwise?' The lines have indeed a powerful simplicity, deriving from an unquestioning confidence (perhaps the Knight's rather than Chaucer's) in the way people ought to behave and do behave. The confidence is expressed in the form of explicit statement in line 903.

895–6. Lines which embody characteristically medieval assumptions about society and the way people behave. They are *gentil* both in their nobility of character and in their being of high social rank: *gentillesse* is simultaneously an ethical and a social concept. And *love*, for courtly ladies, is necessarily the most admirable and deserving of motives for a fight.

897. *saugh* The subject of this verb is *the ladies* of line 893.

898. *bothe lasse and moore* Literally, 'of lower and higher rank', but a common tag in Middle English verse used simply as an emphatic way of saying 'all'.

903. This identical line is used by Chaucer in three other places in his work. As was remarked in the note on lines 55–6, pity is an emotion admired by Chaucer, and by medieval writers generally.

908. *in his resoun* 'when he considered it reasonably'.

920. *that he first bigan* 'the offence he originally committed'.

922. *kan no divisioun* 'recognize no distinction'.

927–77. This long speech by Theseus, which was largely invented by Chaucer, begins as an assertion of the power of the god of love, and as such became famous among later poets in the courtly tradition; indeed its opening lines are sometimes quoted word for word. But the speech develops later in a somewhat unexpected way; for the power it attributes to love is a power to make his followers behave like fools; and this disrespectful attitude towards love, emphasized particularly in the animal images of line 952, was less often recalled by later poets.

933. *Lo heere* A normal phrase for calling attention to a particular example illustrating some general point.

941. 'There are no true fools but lovers.'

942. *for Goddes sake that sit above* 'for the sake of God, who dwells above'.

943. *be they noght wel arrayed?* 'don't they look splendid?' The question is of course ironic.

946–7. 'And yet those who serve love whatever happens fancy themselves very wise.'

949. *jolitee* 'fun' (again ironic).

950. 'Shows them as little gratitude as she does me.'

952. *a cokkow or an hare* Both traditionally silly creatures.

953. 'But everything has to be tried once, whatever it is.' *Hoot and cold* is probably just an emphatic way of saying 'everything, no matter what' (compare *lasse and moore* in line 898); but it is possible that it refers more specifically to the warmth (or the lack of it) of the love that is being discussed.

955. *myself* 'my own experience'.

956. *a servant was I oon* 'I was one of the god of love's followers'. For *servant* in this sense, compare *servise* and *serven*
in lines 945 and 947. The god of love was conceived of as a
feudal lord, and all lovers were in his service.

965. *night ne day* Another phrase on the pattern of *hoot and
cold*, meaning 'at any time'.

966. *in all that ye may* 'in every way you can'.

968. 'And they promised him faithfully to do as he asked.'

969. 'And begged him for protection and mercy.' They have
put themselves outside the law by their actions, and so they
beg him to become their feudal lord and grant them his
protection.

975. *as for* 'on behalf of'.

979–80. 'One of you, whether he likes it or not, may go and
blow on an ivy leaf, for all the good it will do him.' *Pipen in an
ivy leef* is a proverbial expression (with the country air of most
of Chaucer's proverbs) meaning to do something pointless.
By blowing on a leaf one can make a squeaking noise; but why
the proverb should specify an *ivy* leaf, which would be
poisonous, it is difficult to guess. The rhyming of words of
identical sound but different meaning (like *lief* and *leef*)
was permitted in Middle English, as it is in classical French
verse.

982. 'However jealous or angry you may be.'

986. *youre ende of that* 'the result for you of what'.

987. *for plat conclusioun* 'to make a plain end of the matter'.

989. 'If you find it acceptable, take it as meant for the best.'

992. 'And in a year from today, neither more nor less.'

1002. *to wyve* 'as a wife'. *Wyve* is the inflected dative form of
wyf.

1003. Again Fortune is asserted to be the overruling power of
the action; indeed, Theseus is deliberately abandoning his
power of choice, even while acting so decisively, and is
throwing the event into the hands of Fortune.

1005. 'And as sure as I hope God will have pity on my soul, I
will be an impartial and true judge. The only settlement I will
accept will be the death or capture of one of you.'

1009. *yow thinketh* 'it seems to you'. In Middle English, the
two verbs 'to seem' and 'to think', which in Old English had
had the distinct forms *thynkan* and *thencan* fell together as
thinken. *Thinken* in the sense 'seem' is an impersonal verb, and

since *thinketh* is the third person singular of the present indicative, *yow thinketh* must mean 'it seems to you', not 'you think'.

1011. *youre ende* 'the end of your quarrel'.

1012–16. For the Knight this outburst of joy seems entirely appropriate—Theseus really has done everyone a great favour in arranging that the dispute should be settled by a tournament whose result none can predict—but we are not necessarily intended to share his view. He is inside the world of chivalric romance, but we are outside it, as is Chaucer.

1047. *Doon make* 'had made'. *Oratorie* i.e. a place for prayers.

1054. Diana is the goddess of chastity as well as of hunting.

1055. *doon wroght* 'had made'.

1060. *maystow se* In this section the poem is taking on the characteristically medieval (and particularly late medieval) form of a description of emblematic painting, sculpture, etc. We are taken on a conducted tour of the temples, having their salient features pointed out to us; and because the reality seen is emblematic, what is conveyed is not merely decorative charm or grandeur, but thought about the meaning of the gods and the human passions they stand for. For Chaucer this meaning is more important and more sombre than for Boccaccio; thus he adds lines 1060–6, where we are invited to 'see' unhappy consequences of passionate love which it would in fact be hard to render pictorially, and lines 1089–94, where the destructive power of love is asserted in a way that does not even pretend to be pictorial.

1066. 'The oaths with which they support their promises.'

1067–9. Note the apparently casual mixture of good and bad qualities among these personifications: Venus, or passionate love, being itself a non-moral impulse, leads to good and bad consequences at random.

1071. The Middle Ages possessed a fixed colour-symbolism in matters connected with love. Yellow symbolized jealousy, blue constancy, green inconstancy, and so on.

1072. The cuckoo no doubt symbolizes the cuckoldry which gives cause for jealousy.

1073. *caroles* Not the same as modern carols, but ring dances accompanied by a song.

1077. *make of mencioun* 'make mention of'.

1078. *Citheroun* Venus was called Cytherea because she was supposed to live in the island of Cythera, but Chaucer, in common with many medieval writers, wrongly associated her with Mount Cithaeron, the home of the Muses.

1082. Idleness keeps the gate of the garden of love in the *Roman de la Rose*. Now begins a list—a favourite device of medieval poetry—of figures from scriptural and classical legend who were especially associated with love.

1083. *Narcisus* Narcissus fell in love with his own reflexion in a pool, and died as a result. The pool of Narcissus is also found in the garden of the *Roman de la Rose*.

1084. *Salomon* Solomon had many wives and concubines, and was led by them into idolatry in his old age, for which his kingdom was punished.

1085. *Ercules* Hercules was famous for his strength, but he also suffered through love, in being killed by a poisoned shirt sent to him out of jealousy by his wife.

1086. *Medea and Circes* Both were enchantresses; Medea used her spells to help Jason, with whom she was in love, to capture the golden fleece, and later murdered their children through jealousy; Circe, with whom Ulysses fell in love, used hers to turn his companions into animals.

1087. *Turnus* Turnus, in Virgil's *Aeneid*, fought Aeneas for the sake of Lavinia, and was killed by him.

1088. *Cresus* Croesus, like the figures mentioned in the few lines preceding, came to a bad end, being overthrown by Cyrus; but why Chaucer thought this had something to do with Venus is not clear.

1089–96. Having gone through the list, Chaucer explicitly draws the moral it implies; the explicit moralizing is as typical of medieval poetry as the encyclopaedic list itself, and so is the assurance that even more *exempla* could be found to prove the same point.

1097–104. Venus was born of the sea, and one of the poses in which she is traditionally represented in medieval and Renaissance art is rising from the sea (Botticelli's *Birth of Venus* is probably the most familiar example nowadays). The pose and her attributes, such as the musical instrument, the roses, and the doves, were formalized in mythological treatises; it was through these, as much as through actual pictures, that the traditional description descended. Treatises that Chaucer may have known are the *De Deorum Imaginibus* of Albericus and Boccaccio's own *De Genealogia Deorum*.

1114. This actual temple is described at length by Statius, and the description is repeated and elaborated by Boccaccio both in the *Teseida* and in the *De Genealogia Deorum*. Chaucer manages to get it in only by making it a picture on the wall of the temple erected by Theseus; but the lack of probability of this device does not matter, for once again description is made the vehicle for the exposition of ideas.

1116. *mansioun* 'dwelling'; but the word also has an astrological significance, meaning the 'house' or sign of the zodiac which specially belongs to the planet Mars.

1129. *The northren light* The temple is in the cold north (see line 1115), and so the light shining into it will be cold and dim.

1137. *Ther saugh I* This may be the Knight recalling an actual visit to the temple of Mars in Thrace; or it may be the anonymous *persona* of the poet intruding accidentally because such allegorical sights tended to be seen (in a dream, for example) by the 'I' of medieval poetry.

1137–8. *the derke imagining* of treachery is its obscure conception in the mind; *the compassing* of it is its bringing to pass in action.

1159. *shippes hoppesteres* A famous example of an apparent misunderstanding by Chaucer of his sources. Statius has *bellatrices carinae* and Boccaccio *navi bellatrici*, both meaning 'warships', but Chaucer appears to have read the imaginary word *ballatrices* or *ballatrici*, meaning 'dancing' (as ships may be said to dance on the waves).

1161. *freten* 'devour'. This is the infinitive, not the present participle, following from *saugh I* two lines back: literally, 'I saw...the sow to eat the child'.

1163. *by the infortune of Marte* 'with reference to the ill-fortune caused by Mars'.

1164. *cartere...carte* Probably 'charioteer...chariot'. *Carte* was used both for 'cart' and for 'chariot', and indeed the very idea of a chariot seems not to have been understood in the Middle Ages, since pictures based on descriptions of people riding chariots (including pictures of Mars himself) tend to show them riding in farm wagons.

1166. *of Martes divisioun* 'under the influence of Mars'.

1167. The barber comes under Mars's influence because medieval barbers also acted as blood-letters and surgeons. The place of the butcher as a shedder of blood is more obvious, and that of the smith is stated in the next line.

1170–2. Conquest is depicted like Damocles, with a symbolic

sword hanging over his head, ready at any moment to deprive him of his glory.

1173–4. Julius Caesar was murdered, Nero and Mark Antony committed suicide.

1177. *right by figure* 'exactly in the diagram', i.e. the astrological diagram or horoscope showing how the stars foretold their deaths.

1187. One method of divination, called geomancy, began by making at random four rows of dots, which were taken as figures symbolic of the positions of the stars. *Puella* and *Rubeus* were the names of two such figures, both of which were sometimes dedicated to Mars.

1189–90. This detail, which was added by Chaucer, is part of a traditional symbolism, for an early etymology of Mars, quoted by Albericus, derives it from *mares vorans*, 'eating males'.

1198–216. The temple of Diana is not described by Boccaccio, and these examples of transformations connected with Diana and chastity are all taken by Chaucer from Ovid's *Metamorphoses*.

1198–201. Callisto was transformed by Diana into a bear, and the bear was transformed by Jupiter into the constellation called the Great Bear. The pole-star, however, is in the Little Bear, and Chaucer may not fully have understood the legend.

1203. Callisto's son, Arcas, was transformed into the constellation Boötes.

1204–6. Daphne, the daughter of Peneus, a river-god, was transformed into a laurel tree when being pursued by Apollo, who loved her.

1207–10. Actaeon was turned into a stag for having seen Diana bathing naked, and was then killed by his own hounds.

1212–13. Atalanta and Meleager hunted and killed a wild boar sent by Diana to ravage Calydon. There are various accounts of the bad end Meleager came to as a result.

1217–28. Once again the details of the description are symbolic rather than evocative. The hart, dogs, bow, and arrows represent Diana's function as goddess of hunting. The moon is there because Diana was also Luna, the moon-goddess. She is looking down to the underworld because she had a third identity as Hecate, goddess of Hades. And the woman in labour is present because Diana had yet another identity as Lucina, goddess of childbirth.

1224. Pluto was ruler of Hades, the underworld of Greek mythology.

Notes

1230. This line is probably not intended to sound as bathetic as it does to modern ears, for in Chaucer's time colours for painting were very expensive, and were often the subject of contracts between artists and patrons.

1232. *his grete cost* 'great expense to himself'.

1246–7. 'Was there such a noble company for its size throughout the whole world created by God.'

1257. *benedicitee* As often, slurred in pronunciation: *ben'citee* or *ben'dis'tee*.

1261–5. *Som* in each of these lines is singular, not plural: 'one'.

1263. *paire plates* 'Pair' is not followed by 'of' in Middle English. *Plates* are steel plates worn one over each breast.

1264. The Knight had himself fought in Prussia (see *General Prologue*, 53), and so this reference to a Prussian shield is appropriate.

1267. Another of the poem's few references to its historical setting (cf. line 135 and note), but one which at the same time illustrates the medieval lack of any sense of the difference of the past from the present. The knights are dressed in a completely medieval way, like those in medieval paintings of historical events.

1270–323. In Boccaccio the whole of one book is occupied with descriptions of the various champions on each side. Chaucer reduces these to two, Lygurge and Emetreus, and borrows details from different portraits in Boccaccio in order to build up his own descriptions. They are arranged with careful symmetry, each being given twenty-seven lines, and the selection of details is highly significant. His descriptive method is that of medieval poetry in general—the exhaustive accumulation of detail rather than the selection of salient points to give a general impression. Here it is seen at its best, for the details combine to create a coherent effect. He lays great stress on the bestial qualities of the two champions: they are like savage animals in their appearance, their dress, and their attendants. Thus the chivalric pageantry orders without concealing or transforming the savage and destructive elements in human life, which are so prominent in the world of the poem. Similar as they are in this respect, the two champions are also clearly differentiated; and it has been suggested that they have an astrological significance, as being types of the man dominated by Saturn and by Mars. Contemporary accounts of the Saturnalian and Martian types do indeed

Notes

share many details of appearance with Lygurge and Emetreus, and their savage qualities would be thoroughly appropriate as amplifications of the ferocity attributed to the planetary gods in *The Knight's Tale*.

1275. A griffin is a fabulous animal, part lion and part eagle. The mixture of savage qualities is entirely appropriate to the method of these portraits.

1297–8. Emetreus seems to have been invented by Chaucer, and the reference to authority in *in stories as men finde* is presumably intended to distract our attention from this fact.

1301. This line supports the astrological interpretation mentioned above.

1302. *clooth of Tars* Rich silk from Turkestan.

1320. Perhaps a falcon is intended.

1329. *alle and some* 'one and all'—another emphatic way of saying 'all'.

1337–8. A good example of the elaborately superlative expressions that the idiom of chivalric romance runs to.

1339–48. An example of the figure of speech called by the medieval rhetoricians *occupatio*, in which the writer refuses to describe or discuss some particular subject. Here it is used not merely functionally, as a means of abbreviation, but with greater sophistication, as a way of evoking the atmosphere of medieval courtly revelry. No doubt Chaucer had in mind the court of Richard II, and his audience would understand this.

1342. At a medieval feast, as in some Oxford and Cambridge colleges today, the guests would be seated at the High Table on the dais in strict order of seniority.

1350. As usual, the rhetorical devices of Chaucer's style are directed specifically at his audience: he draws their attention to the fact that now something important is going to happen.

1356–7. The language of Christian devotion is applied to the pagan goddess.

1357. *Citherea* See note on line 1078.

1359. *in hir houre* That is, in the hour belonging to Venus. For astrological purposes, day and night were each divided into twelve 'hours' (which would actually only have been an hour long when the days and nights were of equal length), and the first hour after sunrise on each day was dedicated to the planet after whom the day was named. Each following 'unequal' hour was dedicated to another planet according to the order of the distance of the seven planets from the earth.

The first hour of Sunday would belong to the sun, and the second to Venus; the ninth, sixteenth and twenty-third hours would also belong to Venus. Palamon rose two hours before sunrise, which would be in the twenty-third hour, and thus in the hour of Venus.

1364. Venus was the daughter of Jupiter, the father of the gods, and was married to Vulcan, the deformed smith of the gods.

1365. *Citheron* See note on line 1078.

1366. Venus loved Adonis, and when he was killed by a boar she fell into intense grief.

1378. The descent in this line from the dignified language used earlier in his prayer is no doubt deliberate: we are to be reminded of what devotion to Venus would mean in practice. Palamon is at once a pagan and a medieval courtly lover—indeed the suggestion is doubtless that courtly love is a form of paganism—and in his devotion there is a comic extravagance, since its object is to destroy chastity.

1384-5. This is once again perhaps intended to be comically unheroic. *Die in thy servise* is a significantly vague phrase: does it mean simply to die peacefully, married to Emelye rather than in battle, or does it mean to die while actually making love to Emelye?

1390. *so be* 'it may be true'.

1394. *where I ride or go* 'whether I ride or walk', i.e. at all times.

1413. For *houre inequal*, see note on line 1359.

that 'from the time when'. Palamon rose on the twenty-third hour of Sunday; the third 'unequal hour' from that, counting inclusively, would be the first 'unequal hour' of Monday. This would be dedicated to the god after whom Monday was named—that is, Diana, the moon-goddess, to whom Emelye prays.

1419. *clothes* In Boccaccio Emilia puts on a splendid purple robe after washing herself, and this is presumably what is referred to, although it might be the hangings mentioned in line 1423.

1427. 'Unless I were to say something of it in general terms.'

1430. Probably, 'But it is a good thing for one to be left free to imagine it.' Quite what is hinted at in this and the last two lines is not clear. There is presumably some suggestion that the rites performed before Diana by a pagan girl might be indecent; at least there is an odd prurience in the Knight's attitude which once again detracts from the high dignity of the ceremonies in this part.

1436. *Stace of Thebes* 'the *Thebaid* of Statius'. Statius does not in fact describe Emelye's sacrifice, but he does describe other pagan rites, and the addition of *and thise bookes olde* indicates that the *Thebaid* is only being mentioned as one example of the old books where one would be able to read more about pagan ceremonies.

1441. See note on lines 1217–28 and 1224.

1444. *As keepe* 'keep'. The *as* is a normal way of introducing a request. See lines 1459–67.

1445. See note on lines 1207–10.

1451. The alliteration supports the lyrical evocativeness of the line.

1455. Horace calls Diana *diva triformis*, 'three-natured goddess', the three natures referred to being as Diana on earth, Luna in heaven, and Hecate in Hades. See note on lines 1217–28.

1464. *do me grace* 'grant me favour'.

1470. 'Since thou art a virgin and guardian of all of us virgins.'

1472. *a maide* 'as a virgin'.

1482. *As it were* 'something like'. The bloody drops no doubt symbolize the loss of virginity.

1497–9. This has in fact already happened. In Boccaccio Diana's speech comes first and the omen afterwards, and Chaucer seems to have forgotten that he has reversed the order of events.

1509. See note on line 1359. Mars's next hour would have been the fourth after sunrise.

1518. 'Complete control of all warfare.'

1527–32. Mars had a secret love affair with Venus, but Vulcan, her husband, trapped the two of them together in a net.

1530. 'Although on one occasion it went amiss with you.'

1536–7. 'And as I believe, more injured by love than ever any creature alive has been.'

1551. 'To do your will and act according to your powerful skills.'

1575. *seyde* 'it said'.

1579. His delight is expressed in the jaunty rhythm and alliteration of the line; and it contrasts with the dolefulness with which the promise of victory is given.

1588. 'By which he soon satisfied each party.'

1589–91. A characteristic Chaucerian pause to insert a generalizing *sententia* in justification of the particular event narrated.

1593. 'Although it is against his nature', Saturn's nature being to produce disasters, as was suggested by Arcite in lines 229–31, and as Saturn himself goes on to indicate in detail.

1595. Venus was Saturn's granddaughter, but is called his daughter in *Roman de la Rose*.

1596. Of the seven 'planets' known in the Middle Ages, Saturn had the widest orbit.

1598. *wan* Like many medieval colour-adjectives, *wan* expresses a particular emotional intensity rather than a precise tint. It means something like 'gloomy'—at once pale and dark, like lead. Here it seems to be applied to the sea, and appropriately, since drowning would be most likely to take place in a storm. But *wan* would also fit the appearance of the drowned man himself.

1599. In the Middle Ages (and in Shakespeare's time—see *Twelfth Night*) madmen were imprisoned in a dark house, and this may be referred to here.

1601. Chaucer and his audience would no doubt have had in mind the Peasants' Revolt of 1381.

1604. Leo is the sign of the zodiac opposite to Saturn's own house of Aquarius; in it he is as malignant as in his own house, and his strength is increased by that of the lion.

1608. Samson destroyed the Philistines, who had imprisoned him, by pulling down the supports of the temple where he was displayed, but in doing so killed himself too.

1610. 'The secret acts of treachery and the long-laid plots.'

1617–18. 'Although you are not of the same disposition, which is what causes such constant disagreement.'

1635–825. The details of the tournament, like those of the poem's other events, are completely medieval; and, to a greater extent than Boccaccio's, Chaucer's description can be paralleled throughout from contemporary historians such as Froissart.

1633–64. For comment on this scene, see Introduction, pp. 42–3.

1643–5. Here three ranks are distinguished among the participants: *lordes* who are independent, *knightes of retenue* who are in the service of the *lordes*, and *squieres* who serve both.

1645. *Nailinge the speres* Fastening the heads to the shafts.

1652. *thikke as they may goon* 'clustered as densely as possible'.

1654. *blody sounes* 'calls to bloodshed'.

1656. 'Three in one place, ten in another, conducting discussions.'

1658. 'Some said one thing, some said another.'

1659. *him* 'the one'.

1661. *he...he* 'this one...that one'.

1677. *the peple of noise al stille* 'that the noise of the people was completely silenced'.

1694. *stake* A palisade, within which the prisoners on each side are to be kept.

1705-6. There is perhaps implied a contrast between this 'lord', who has previously been described as sitting like *a god in trone* (line 1671), and the actual gods of the poem, who do seem to desire bloodshed. There is at least a general contrast, which these lines help to build up, between Theseus, the human ruler who attempts to control the savage elements in human life, and the gods, who are the very expression of those savage elements.

1710. *and nat with sarge* Serge, a thick, hard-wearing cloth, is mentioned as a contrast with cloth of gold, which would be decorative and expensive, but not serviceable.

1721. *in degrees* 'on the steps'. As described in lines 1032-3, the lists were constructed with stepped seats round them, so that the watchers could see over each others' heads.

1723. *Marte* i.e. the statue of Mars, before which Arcite had made his prayer.

1729. 'If one were to search up and down throughout the whole world.'

1735. *for to gesse* 'to judge by conjecture'—without actually counting and examining them.

1738. 'So that there should be no deception as to their numbers.' It had been agreed that there should be exactly a hundred on each side.

1744. *in arrest* The spears were very long, and were held steady in a rest attached to the saddle.

1748. *He* 'one man'.

1749. This and the preceding line mention the two consequences of the line before them: the spears splinter on the shields, one man is stabbed in the stomach by a spear, and pieces of broken spears fly twenty feet into the air. Then in the next line, having used their spears, they go on to the next stage of the battle, with swords. A general mêlée ensues.

1754. *He* 'one man'.

1756-9. *He...He...he him...He* 'one knight...a second...a third...a fourth...one'.

1762. 'Another is also led to the "stake" on the other side.'

1766. *his felawe* 'each other'.

1768–71. This comparison was added by Chaucer, and there seems no reason for mentioning *Galgopheye* (Gargaphia in Boeotia), except that it was where Actaeon was turned into a stag, and was therefore associated by Chaucer with hunting—hence the hunter is mentioned as the tiger's prey. Together with the comparison of the lion, which follows, and was also added by Chaucer, it forms a deliberately symmetrical pair, recalling lines 797–801, in which Arcite was also compared to a tiger and Arcite to a lion. The lion and the tiger are conventional symbols of savage cruelty, ungoverned by reason, and they are part of a whole train of wild beast imagery in the poem, whose function is to suggest the savage element which lies close beneath the surface of human life.

1772. *Belmarye* Benmarin, in North Africa. In *The General Prologue* we are told that the Knight had himself been there.

1793. 'Because they were too strong for him and also because it was part of the agreement.'

1808. In the form of rain.

1816. Suggested by the noise of the trumpeters and heralds, but addressed to the audience of pilgrims—' *You* be quiet too.'

1823–4. These lines do not occur in the best manuscripts, but they seem thoroughly Chaucerian. They explain what in a 'pure' chivalric romance would remain unexplained and would not seem to need explanation, and in doing so they cast a quizzical glance on the conventions of romance itself.

1825. Probably 'And was all his delight, so far as his heart was concerned.' But the reading of the line is doubtful, some manuscripts having *and* for *as*, and so is its interpretation.

1838. By cutting the straps that held the armour together.

1852. 'Who had his breast-bone pierced with a spear.'

1854. *charmes* 'incantations'. Medieval medicine, though elaborately developed as a theory (see lines 1885–900 below), was by modern standards a pseudo-science, employing some of the methods of magic.

1865–7. 'Nor (is it more than an accident) for one single person, without help, to be taken prisoner by twenty knights and, without surrendering, to be led by force to the "stake".'

1871. 'It was not imputed as any dishonour to him.' *Vileynye* is the behaviour or qualities of character to be expected of a *vileyn*, a person of the lower classes. The medieval assumption was that, ideally, noble qualities of character went with noble birth, and *vice versa*. See *An Introduction to Chaucer*, Appendix.

1873. *leet crye* 'had proclaimed'.

1875. This proclamation of the equal success of both sides, together with his earlier refusal to worry people by abandoning the festivities, helps to establish Theseus as a symbol of rational rule, struggling against the passions that turn men into beasts.

1885–900. Most of these medical details were added by Chaucer, partly no doubt because he was interested in the sciences, but also because they increase the horror and inevitability of Arcite's death.

1887. *for any lechecraft* 'for all that medical skill can do'.

1889. *veine-blood* ('blood-letting') was a favourite remedy for almost any illness in medieval times and later. A vein was opened and the blood allowed to flow out.

ventusinge ('cupping') was a way of removing blood from some part of the body by applying a vacuum to a nearby part.

1891–3. The animal virtue, one of the three virtues mentioned in the note on lines 511–18, controlled the action of the muscles, including those that govern breathing. One of its functions was to expel impurities from the natural virtue through the lungs; but in Arcite's case the lungs were damaged, and so the impurities collected in them and caused his death.

1901–2. No doubt this was a proverb: where the forces of the body itself will not help, medical treatment is of so little use that you might as well bury the sick person at once.

1903. *This* 'this is'—common abbreviated form in Middle English.

al and som 'the long and short of it'.

1908. *o point* 'a single part'.

1913–24. This formal lamentation by Arcite is a perfect example of how the devices of medieval rhetoric enable poetry to achieve by non-naturalistic means moving effects that pure naturalism would find impossible. With the effect of changes of key in music, the rhetoric moves from plangent mourning over his own situation to a piercingly compressed summary of the human situation in general, and from that to a renewed intimacy.

1917. *wyf* In Boccaccio Arcite had gone through a form of marriage with Emelye immediately after the tournament; but Chaucer's retention of the word is surely not mere carelessness, for it is particularly moving that Arcite should call her wife for the first time when death makes it impossible to hope that he will marry her. Similarly in Shakespeare's play, Cleopatra calls Antony husband for the first time as she is about to die.

1918. *endere of my lyf* 'cause of my death'.

1921. This line, which comes so movingly at this particular point, appears to have been a formula in Middle English, and was used by Chaucer himself elsewhere—in *The Miller's Tale*, for example, to remark how the scholar Nicholas had lodgings by himself.

1922. *sweete foo* This and other oxymorons are commonly used in medieval literature to describe the paradoxical effect of love. Here the phrase takes on new meaning, for Emelye is his enemy in causing not the metaphorical 'death' of the lover but his real death.

1928. Compare line 1005 and note.

1929–30. 'So far as true lovers are concerned, with all the attributes proper to them.' *Servaunt* is here used in the specialized sense of line 956, to mean a follower of the god of love. *Service* in line 1910 above may have an undertone of the same meaning.

1931–3. These are the qualities traditionally attributed to the medieval courtly lover. *Heigh kinrede*, 'noble relations'; *that art*, 'the art of love'.

1934. 'May Jupiter protect my soul'—a repetition of the asseveration of line 1928, after the parenthesis.

1943. *And yet mooreover for* 'and all the more because'.

1945. *withouten moore* 'and that alone'.

1946. According to medieval physiology, the heart, and not the brain, was the seat of the intellect.

1951–78. After the unflawed pathos of Arcite's death, Chaucer seems to retreat from seriousness into something almost like burlesque. This is observable first in the Knight's refusal of theological speculation about the destination of Arcite's soul—a subject on which Chaucer has sly remarks elsewhere in his works, usually making the point that those who argue so knowingly about the after-life are necessarily arguing from a total lack of experience. Next there seems to be some deliberate exaggeration in the shrieking and howling of Emelye and Palamon; though it is difficult to be certain about this, since, as has been remarked elsewhere, emotions are generally presented in a conventionally intensified form in this poem, and the word 'howl' may possibly have sounded less undignified in Chaucer's time than it does now. There is surely some Chaucerian slyness, though, in lines 1964–8: we are not necessarily to share the Knight's confidence in his generalization about women, especially since Emelye does not die of grief, but lives to marry Palamon. And finally the sorrow of the women is again debased by their linking of gold and Emelye in line 1978, in a way which makes Emelye sound almost an afterthought.

1952. 'Whose whereabouts, since I have never been there, I cannot tell.' In Boccaccio, Arcite's soul ascends to the eighth sphere of the heavens—a passage which Chaucer had already made use of in describing the end of Troilus in *Troilus and Criseyde*. It is not only for this reason, though, that he does not use it again here; for in *The Knight's Tale* he does not wish to identify the pagan 'theology' of the poem with the Christian theology in which he and his audience believed. The imaginative world of *The Knight's Tale* is crueller than the world of medieval Christianity.

1954. 'I find nothing concerning souls in the contents of my book.' As he habitually does, Chaucer is treating his source equivocally; for, as remarked in the previous note, his main source does say something about the fate of Arcite's soul.

1957. 'May Mars direct his soul!' Boccaccio had referred to Mercury, but Chaucer wishes to insert a last reminder of Arcite's dedication to Mars, which has caused his death.

1960–1. *Theseus his suster took anon Swowninge* 'Theseus immediately seized his sister-in-law as she fainted'.

1974–5. When Hector, the greatest warrior of the Trojans, and son of King Priam, was killed in battle by the Greek Achilles, there was great sorrow at his death. Such comparisons with events from classical legend are a common means of heightening emotion at crucial points in medieval poems. The story of the Trojan war, particularly, provided a universal standard of judgement for medieval poets and their audiences.

1977. *woldestow be deed* 'wouldst thou die'—as we should say, 'why did you have to die'.

1990. This line comes home more powerfully because it is addressed to an audience who really are pilgrims.

1997–8. *may best ymaked be, And eek moost honurable in his degree* 'might be held best and most suitably to his rank'.

2007. *leet comande* 'had orders given'.

2012–13. *ysent After* 'sent for'.

2019. *bare the visage* 'with his face bare'.

2027. *passinge othere of wepinge* 'weeping more than the others'.

2031. *leet forth thre steedes bringe* 'had three war-horses brought out'.

2037. *bowe Turkeys* 'Turkish bow'—distinctively curved and richly ornamented.

2056. *fyr-makinge* 'making of the pyre'.

2061–106. An extraordinarily long *occupatio*, which does indeed abbreviate Boccaccio's description, but which would no doubt also be admired as a piece of rhetorical virtuosity.

2063–5. Lists of trees are a common convention of medieval (and classical) poetry. Chaucer would have found lists both in the *Teseida* and in the *Thebaid*, as well as in Ovid and other poets, and he gives another list himself in *The Parliament of Fowls*.

2067. *the goddes* The spirits who in classical mythology were supposed to live in the woods, and who are enumerated in line 2070.

2070. Nymphs is strictly the generic name for local deities; fauns are half men, half goats; and hamadryads are tree-gods.

2100. It was the custom in Chaucer's time (as in some places now) to stay up at night with the dead body.

2102. *wake-pleyes* In classical times a funeral was celebrated with games; and in medieval England the *lyche-wake* was sometimes interrupted with games. Chaucer seems to be fusing together the two customs.

2118. 'Had the noble Palamon sent for.'

2119. *Unwist of him* 'without his knowing'.

2129–58. The first thirty lines of Theseus's speech are not found in Boccaccio. They are largely made up of ideas and phrases taken from Boethius, as can be illustrated by quotation from Chaucer's own translation of the *De Consolatione*. It is argued in the Introduction (pp. 75–8), however, that the speech cannot be taken simply as an exposition of Boethian philosophy, explaining the principle of order in the universe in answer to Palamon's arraignment of divine providence at the end of Book I, and fitting all the events of the Tale into a philosophical pattern. The speech expresses the difficulty philosophy has in ordering the universe: it begins confidently, but gradually loses itself in embarrassedly over-assertive repetitions, and eventually moves away from metaphysics altogether, turning to 'philosophy' of another kind—practical wisdom about how to live in *this wrecched world*.

2129. In medieval philosophy God is conceived of both as the 'First Mover' of the universe, who sets the spheres in motion, and as its 'First Cause', on which it depends for its existence.

2130. Boethius sees the world as governed by a bond of love; and in the *Roman de la Rose* Nature, God's vice-gerent, keeps in being a golden chain which binds together the four elements, the basic units of matter.

2131. A line with a confident swing, which anticipates the Augustan heroic line in its balance. The confidence is continued in the alliteration of the next line.

2141. 'Although they may indeed cut those days short.'

2142-3. Cf. note on lines 465-6.

2147. 'Anyone except a fool can easily understand.'

2155. *speces* A technical term of medieval philosophy—'kinds'. *progressiouns* Perhaps 'things proceeding from sources'.

2156-7. *by successiouns, And nat eterne* 'in succession to one another and not each eternally'.

2159. Here Chaucer returns from Boethius to Boccaccio.

2168. *al this thing* 'everything' (also in line 2176).

2169. *Of man and womman* 'so far as men and women are concerned'.

2172. *He moot be deed* 'they must die'. The reference to medieval society was added by Chaucer.

2174. *large feeld* Perhaps 'field of battle', in which case *as men may see* would mean 'as we have seen'.

2177. Here the planetary god is substituted for the Christian God; but the grafting is hardly satisfactory, since we have already seen that a world governed by the planetary gods is in effect a world governed by Fortune; and we have seen too how ineffectual the benevolent Jupiter is compared with the more sinister god Saturn.

2183-5. Here is the turning-point of the speech, at which it abandons the attempt to make the universe rational, and turns to an attempt to give advice about how to live in an irrational universe.

2186. 'And especially what is due to all of us'—that is, death.

2188. *him that al may gye* 'him who has power to control everything'—that is, Jupiter.

2192. *him* 'himself'.

2203. Life as a prison is a familiar conception of medieval and earlier philosophy, but here it takes on a more specific meaning from the material prison in which both knights have earlier been kept, and from which they have been released. The release was only apparent; life itself is a prison.

2206. *Kan he hem thank?* 'does he show them any gratitude?'

2218. He has to bear in mind that the marriage of two persons of such high rank is of public importance.

2225. 'Let a proof of your feminine pity now be seen.'

2227. *bacheler* A probationer knight—a man who was training for knighthood but had not yet attained it.

2231. A final application of Christian theology to courtly love; just as God's mercy overcomes his justice in saving mankind, so the lady's mercy must offer the knight what he can never deserve by way of justice—herself.

2241–2. 'And may God, who created this whole wide world, send his love to Palamon, who paid dearly for it.' With these lines we are smoothly returned from the pagan world of the Tale to the Christian world of the pilgrimage.

SUGGESTIONS FOR FURTHER READING

P. M. Kean, *Chaucer and the Making of English Poetry* (Routledge and Kegan Paul), vol. II, pp. 1–52.

Charles Muscatine, *Chaucer and the French Tradition* (University of California Press).

Ian Robinson, *Chaucer and the English Tradition* (Cambridge University Press), pp. 108–46.

Elizabeth Salter, *Chaucer: The Knight's Tale and the Clerk's Tale* (Edward Arnold).

APPENDIX

THE PORTRAIT OF THE KNIGHT IN 'THE GENERAL PROLOGUE'

lines 43–78

A Knight ther was, and that a worthy man,
That fro the time that he first bigan
To riden out, he loved chivalrie,
Trouthe and honour, fredom and curteisie.
Ful worthy was he in his lordes werre,
And therto hadde he riden, no man ferre,
As wel in cristendom as in hethenesse,
And evere honoured for his worthiness.
At Alisaundre he was whan it was wonne.
Ful ofte time he hadde the bord bigonne
Aboven alle nacions in Pruce;
In Lettow hadde he reysed and in Ruce,
No Cristen man so ofte of his degree.
In Gernade at the seege eek hadde he be
Of Algezir, and riden in Belmarye.
At Lyeys was he and at Satalye,
Whan they were wonne; and in the Grete See
At many a noble armee hadde he be.
At mortal batailles hadde he been fiftene,
And foughten for oure feith at Tramissene
In listes thries, and ay slain his foo.
This ilke worthy knight hadde been also
Sometime with the lord of Palatye
Again another hethen in Turkye.
And everemoore he hadde a sovereyn prys;
And though that he were worthy, he was wys,

And of his port as meeke as is a maide.
He nevere yet no vileinye ne saide
In al his lif unto no maner wight.
He was a verray, parfit gentil knight.
But, for to tellen yow of his array,
His hors were goode, but he was nat gay.
Of fustian he wered a gipon
Al bismotered with his habergeon,
For he was late ycome from his viage,
And wente for to doon his pilgrimage.

GLOSSARY

a a; in

abide(n) wait for, remain
(l. 2124) waited

aboght (inf. *abyen*) paid for

abood delay

aboughte (inf. *abyen*) (l. 1445)
suffered

aboute (l. 32) in turn;
(l. 1029) around;
(l. 284) *been aboute* be
getting ready.

above (l. 1045) in the upper
part; (l. 2129) in the
heavens

aboven (l. 1911) before

abregge (inf. *abreggen*) cut
short

accomplice (inf. *accomplicen*)
accomplish

accord agreement

accused (inf. *accusen*) blamed

acorded (inf. *acorden*) agreed

Adoon Adonis

adoun down, down here

afered afraid

affermed (inf. *affermen*)
decreed

after afterwards, after,
according to

again, ageyn again, in return,
in reply; (l. 1593) against;
(l. 1822) upon

agast(e) (inf. *agasten*) terri-
fied; (l. 1566) *him agaste*
was frightened

ago(o)n gone (away); ago;
(l. 1926) *many a day agon*
for many days past

agreved (inf. *agreven*)
offended

aiel grandfather

al (adv.) all; very much

al (as conj. followed by subj.
verb) although

alauntz mastiffs

alight (inf. *alighten*) arrived

alighte (inf. *alighten*)
dismounted

alle and some one and all

als as

alwey always

amadrides hamadryads

amende(d) (inf. *amenden*)
(l. 52) put right; (l. 2208)
correct

amenden (l. 2216) reform
ourselves

amiddes in the middle

amorwe next day

amounteth (inf. *amounten*)
means

Amphioun Amphion

an on

a-night at night

animal see note on ll. 1891–3

ano(o)n at once

Antonius Mark Antony

apalled (inf. *apallen*) dimmed

apayd (inf. *apayen*) satisfied

apparaillinge preparation

appetites desires

Argus see note on ll. 527–34

armes arms, warfare; armour;
(l. 154) *in oon armes*, in the
same armour

arm-greet as thick as his arm

193

armipotente powerful in arms

array condition; dress; decoration

arrayed (ll. 1188, 1232, 2009) arranged; (l. 948) *be they noght wel arrayed?* don't they look splendid?

arreest detention

arrest (l. 1744) rest

arretted (inf. *arretten*) imputed

ars-metrike arithmetic

artow (inf. *been*) art thou

arwes arrows

arys (inf. *arysen*) rise up

as as; as if; like

ashamed (inf. *ashamen*) humiliated

aside to one side

asketh (inf. *asken*) demands

aslaked (inf. *aslaken*) abated

aspect position of planets in relation to each other

assaut assault, direct attack

assayed (inf. *assayen*) tried

asseged (inf. *assegen*) besieged

assent (l. 2111) consent; (l. 2217) opinion; (l. 87) *by noon assent* on any terms

asshen ashes

asshy ash-covered

assuren (inf. *assuren*) (l. 1066) support

assureth (inf. *assuren*) (l. 68) makes secure

astert (inf. *asterten*) escaped

asterte (inf. *asterten*) escape

astoned dumbfounded

atones simultaneously

atrede (inf. *atreden*) outwit

atrenne (inf. *atrennen*) outrun

atte at the

atteyne (inf. *atteynen*) attain

Atthalante Atalanta

atthamaunt adamant

Atthenes Athens, Athenians

Attheon Actaeon

auctoritee authority

aught something, anything

aungel angel

auter altar

availleth (inf. *availlen*) it avails

ava(u)ntage advantage

aventure accident; chance; lot; event; (l. 302) *myn aventure* what had happened to me; (l. 328) *his aventure* what comes to him; (l. 1499) *thyn aventure of love* what will happen to you in love

avis opinion

avow vow

axe (inf. *axen*) ask

axing request

ay ever, always

ayeyn (l. 34) again; (l. 651) towards

ayeyns against

ba(a)r (inf. *beren*) carried; *bar him* conducted himself, acquitted himself; (l. 547) *bar him lowe* acted humbly

bacheler see note on l. 2227

bad (inf. *bidden*) told

balled bald (man)

bane (l. 239) death; (l. 823) killer

bar see *ba(a)r*

barbour barber

bareyne devoid, empty; barren

baronage assembly of barons

bataille battle

bauderie gaiety

bay bay-coloured (i.e. reddish-brown)

be (inf. *been*) are

be(e)n (inf. *been*) are, be

beere bier

beest animal

beete (inf. *be(e)ten*) kindle

Belmarye Benmarin

benedicite praise the Lord!

benigne kind

bente slope

berd beard

ber(e) (inf. *beren*) carry; (l. 1398) pierce; *bere him* behave

bere (noun) bear

bibledde covered with blood

bide (inf. *biden*) wait

bifel (inf. *bifallen*) (it) happened

bifor(e)n before, at the front, in front of

bigonne (inf. *biginnen*) begun

bihoold (inf. *biholden*) look, behold

bihote (inf. *bihoten*) promise

biknowe (inf. *biknowen*) acknowledge

biraft (inf. *bireven*) taken away

biseken beseech

biside alongside

bisily diligently

bisy (l. 633) lively; (ll. 1462, 1584, 1995) anxious

bisynesse industry, diligence (l. 1070) anxiety

bitinge (inf. *biten*) piercing

bitwix(e)(n) between

biwreye (inf. *biwreyen*) disclose

blede (inf. *bleden*) bleed

bleynte (inf. *blenchen*) started back

blisful blessed

blisfully joyfully

blis(se) happiness, blessedness

blody bloody

blood (l. 160) family; (l. 472) race, people; (l. 725) kinsman

blowen (inf. *blowen*) proclaimed

blyve quickly

bocher butcher

bokeling buckling

boket bucket

boles bulls

bond (noun) agreement

bond (inf. *binden*) bound

boon bone

boone prayer, request

boor boar

bore (inf. *beren*) born

bores boars

born (inf. *beren*) borne, carried

borwe (l. 764) *leyd to borwe* pledged

bouk trunk

bounden (inf. *binden*) bound

boundes limits

bowes boughs

brak (inf. *breken*) broke out of

brawnes muscles

brede breadth

breke (inf. *breken*) break

breme furiously

brend burnished

brendest (inf. *brennen*) didst burn

brenninge burning

brenningly fiercely

brent(e) (inf. *brennen*) burnt
breres briars
brest (noun) breast
brest (inf. *bresten*) burst
bresten break
bret-ful brim-full
briddes birds
bridel bridle
brighte beautiful
brode broad
broghte (inf. *bringen*) brought
broided braided
brondes logs; (l. 1481)
    brondes ende end of the
    piece of burning wood
browdinge embroidery
bulte (inf. *bilden*) built
burned burnished
busk(es) bush(es)
but but; unless; only;
    (l. 1387) if
by and by side by side
byjaped (inf. *byjapen*) tricked
caas see *cas*
Cadme, Cadmus Cadmus
Callistope Callisto
cam (inf. *comen*) came
cantel portion
care sorrow
careful sorrowful
careyne corpse
carieden (inf. *carien*) carried
caroles ring dances
carte chariot
cartere charioteer
cas, caas chance, case,
    matter, event; (l. 553)
    affairs; (ll. 1222, 2038)
    quiver; (l. 1964) cases;
    (l. 2113) matters
caste (inf. *casten*) (l. 1313)
    reckon; (l. 1996) considered

castes plots
caughte (inf. *cacchen*) seized
cause (l. 1630) *by the cause*
    that because
caytyf wretched
caytyves wretches, miserable
    creatures
cerial evergreen
certes certainly
certeyn (l. 281) without
    doubt
chambre (small) room,
    bedroom
champartie (l. 1091) *holde*
    champartie share in power
char chariot
charge (l. 426) *thou yevest*
    litel charge you care very
    little; (l. 1429) *it were no*
    charge it would be of little
    importance
charitee kindness; (l. 863)
    charity
charmes incantations
chasteyn chestnut
chaunce accident
chaungen change
cheere expression
che(e)s (inf. *chesen*) choose
cherles of the lower classes
    (see Appendix to *An Intro-*
    duction to Chaucer)
cheyne chain
chiere bearing; (l. 1825) see
    note
chirche church
chirking grating
chivalrie knightly
    accomplishments; company
    of knights
Circes Circe
circuit circumference

circumstances (ll. 1074, 1930)
  attributes; (l. 1405)
  ceremonies
citee city
Citherea Cytherea (see note
  on l. 1078)
Citheroun Cithaeron (but see
  note on l. 1078)
citole a musical instrument
  played by plucking its
  strings
citrin greenish-yellow
clariounis clarions (shrill,
  narrow-tubed trumpets)
clarree drink of sweetened
  wine
clause (l. 905) *shortly in a*
  clause in a short while
Clemence mercy
clene clean, pure
cleped (inf. *clepen*) called
clepen call
clerk learned person, scholar
  (see Appendix to *An Intro-*
  duction to Chaucer)
cloke cloak
clothered clotted
clothes (l. 1423) hangings
cloven (inf. *cleven*) split
cokkow cuckoo
colde cheerless
cole coal
colered of gold with gold
  collars
colpons pieces
comen (inf. *comen*) come
commune in commune com-
  monly, in general
communes common people
compaignye company;
  (l. 1916) companionship,
  intimacy

compas circle
compassing accomplishment
compleccioun disposition
compleyne (inf. *compleynen*)
  lament
compleyninge of lamenting
compleynte lamentation
composicioun agreement
concluden sum up
conclusioun judgement
condicioun character
confort comfort
conforteth (inf. *conforten*)
  comforts
confus distraught
confusioun destruction
conseil (l. 283) *of my conseil*
  in my confidence; (l. 289)
  confidant; (l. 725) *to my*
  conseil sworn sworn to keep
  my confidence; (l. 2238)
  council
conserve (inf. *conserven*)
  preserve
considered (inf. *consideren*)
  taken account of
constellacioun position of
  planets at time of man's
  birth
contek strife
contenaunce appearance
contrarie opponent
contree country
convertinge (inf. *converten*)
  turning back
conveyed (inf. *conveyen*)
  escorted
coppes cups
corage heart, spirits
coroune crown
correccioun punishment
corrumpable corruptible

corrupcioun (l. 1896) putre-
faction
cosin friend
cote cottage
cote-armures jackets worn
over armour to display
heraldic devices
couched (l. 1308) studded;
(l. 2075) laid
cours pursuit; (l. 1596)
orbit; (l. 1691) charge
courser war-horse, charger
covenant(z) promise(s),
agreement(s)
cowardye cowardice
cracchinge (inf. *cracchen*)
scratching
craftes skills
Cresus Croesus
cridestow? (inf. *crien*) didst
thou cry?
cri(e)de(n) (inf. *crien*) cried,
shouted
crope treetop
cry outcry
Cupide, Cupido Cupid
cure care, attention
dampned condemned
Dane Daphne
dar (inf. *daren*) dare,
venture
darreyne (inf. *darreynen*)
settle (the right to)
darst (inf. *daren*) darest
dart arrow, spear
daun see note on l. 521
daunger obligation
daweth (inf. *dawen*) dawns
day (ll. 310, 1618) *al day*
constantly
debaat conflict
debonaire meek

declare (inf. *declaren*) express
decree enactment
dede (noun) deed, action
deduyt pleasure
deed, dede (adj.) dead;
(l. 720) deathly
deedly deathlike
deel (ll. 967, 1233) *every deel*
completely; (l. 2206) *never
a deel* not at all
deeth death
defye (inf. *defyen*) repudiate
degree rank, state of life;
(l. 983) situation; (ll. 1032,
1033, 1721) step; (l. 1334)
at his degree according to
his rank; (l. 1721) *in degrees*
on the steps
delit delight
deme(th) (inf. *demen*) judge,
decide, consider
departe(d) (inf. *departen*)
separate(d)
departinge splitting up
depe (l. 274) solemnly
depeynted (inf. *depeynten*)
depicted
dere (inf. *deren*) trouble
derke dark, obscure
derknesse darkness
derre hath derre loves
more
desiringe desire
despence extravagance
despit malice
despitous angry, contemp-
tuous
desplayeth (inf. *desplayen*)
unfurls
destreyneth (inf. *destreynen*)
afflicts
deth death

devisinge provision

devoir duty

devyse, divyse (inf. *devysen*) (ll. 136, 1056) describe; (ll. 396, 932, 986, 1043) plan; (ll. 558, 567) order

deys dais

Diane Diana

diapred having diaper patterns

diched moated

dide(n) (inf. *doon*) did, made, performed

dight (inf. *dighten*) prepared

digne noble

diligence (l. 1612) *doon diligence* take special care

dim faint

dirriveth (inf. *dirriven*) derives

disconfitinge defeat

disconfiture defeat

disconfort grief

disconforten dishearten

disgised disguised

disherited disinherited

disjoint (l. 2104) *in no disjoint* without getting in difficulties

dispeir despair

dispence expenditure

dispitously scornfully

disposicioun (l. 229) position of planet; (l. 520) disposition

disserved (inf. *disserven*) deserved

distreyne (inf. *distreynen*) afflict

divininge (inf. *divinen*) guessing (what will happen to)

divinis theologians

divinistre seer

divisioun (l. 922) distinction; (l. 1166) company; (l. 1618) disagreement

divyse see *devyse*

doghter daughter

dominacioun power

dongeoun keep

do(o)n cause, show, do, perform; done

dooth (inf. *doon*) does, causes, makes

dore(s) door(s)

doun down; (l. 519) *up so doun* upside down

doute doubt; (l. 283) *out of doute* without doubt

doutelees without doubt

dowves doves

drawe (inf. *drawen*) carry

drawen (l. 1216) recall

drede (noun) fear

drede (inf. *dreden*) fear, doubt

dredeful full of dread

drenching drowning

dresse (inf. *dressen*) (l. 1736) *hem dresse* draw themselves up

dreye dry

dronk drunk

dronken (inf. *drinken*) drank

drugge (inf. *druggen*) (l. 558) *drugge and drawe* fetch and carry

duc ruler

duetee reverence

dure (inf. *duren*) remain, last

dusked (inf. *dusken*) grew dim

dwelleth (inf. *dwellen*) stay(s), remain(s)

dyen die

dys dice

ech(on) each, every
Ector Hector
eek also
eet (inf. *eten*) ate, was eating
effect conclusion, outcome
eft again
Egeus Egeus
eir air
elde old age
elles, ellis else, otherwise
emforth according to
empoisoning poisoning
emprise undertaking
encens incense
enchauntementz magic spells
encombred (inf. *encombren*) burdened
encrees increase
encreeseth (inf. *encressen*) increases
encressen (inf. *encressen*) increase
ende end; (l. 986) result; (l. 1007) settlement
endelong lengthways, the length of
endite write
engendred (inf. *engendren*) produced
enhauncen advance
enhorte (inf. *enhorten*) exhort
enoint (inf. *enointen*) anointed
ensample(s) example(s), illustration(s)
entente intention; (l. 100) *in ful good entente* with good will
entree way in
er before
Ercules Hercules
ere (inf. *eren*) plough
eres ears

ernest earnest
erst than before
erthely earthly, on earth
eschue (inf. *eschuen*) avoid
ese ease
esed (inf. *esen*) comforted
esen (l. 1336) entertain
espye (inf. *espyen*) notice, discover
estaat high rank, condition of life
estres inner rooms
estward to the east
eterne eternal
eve (l. 1963) *bothe eve and morne* all the time
evene (adj.) impartial, equal
evene (adv.) exactly; steadily
evere ever, always; (l. 913) *evere in oon* continually
everemo (for) ever
everich each, every
ew yew
excercise (inf. *excercisen*) display
executeth (inf. *executen*) carries out
expulsif expulsive (see note on ll. 1891-3)
eyen eyes
eyleth (inf. *eylen*) is the matter with
eyr air
fader father
fadme fathoms
faille(n) fail
fain glad(ly)
fair (l. 665) desirable
faire (l. 126) satisfactorily; (l. 1736) properly; (l. 1838) deftly; (l. 968) *faire and weel* faithfully

Glossary

falle (inf. *fallen*) fallen,
  occurred
fallen occur
falle(th) (inf. *fallen*) occur(s)
falow grey
fals(e) false, deceptive,
  unreliable, untrustworthy
fantastik (l. 518) *celle fantastik* cell of perception
fare (noun) (l. 951) goings on
fare (inf. *faren*) travel;
  (l. 1577) *wel to fare* to get
  on well; (l. 1578) gone
faren behave
faste (l. 408) eagerly;
  (ll. 618, 620, 830) close;
  (ll. 1501, 1565) loudly;
  (l. 1700) hard
faught (inf. *fighten*) fought
feeld(es) field(s)
feere fear
fe(e)ste festivity
feith faith, honour
fel (inf. *fallen*) (l. 604)
  happened
felawe member of the company; companion, comrade
felaweshipe companionship
feld (inf. *fellen*) felled
felicitee (true) happiness
fel(le) fierce
felonye treachery
Femenye the country of the
  Amazons
fer far; (l. 790) *as fer as*
  inasmuch as; (l. 992) *fer ne
ner* neither more nor less
ferde(n) (inf. *faren*) acted
fere fear
ferforthly completely
fermacies medicines
ferre further

feste see *feeste*
fet (inf. *fecchen*) fetched
fewe (l. 1247) *of so fewe* for
  its size
fey faith; (l. 265) *by my fey*
  on my honour
fiers fierce
figure (l. 1177) diagram;
  (l. 1185) arrangements
fil(le) (inf. *fallen*) (ll. 176,
  1252) happened; (ll. 245,
  714) fell
fille (noun) (l. 670) *al his fille*
  as much as he wanted
fillen (inf. *fallen*) fell
finde (inf. *finden*) (l. 1555)
  provide
fir fire
firy fiery
fledden (inf. *fleen*) fled
fleen flee, escape from
fleete (inf. *fleten*) float
fletinge (inf. *fleten*) floating
flikeringe (inf. *flikeren*)
  fluttering
florin coin worth 6s. 8d.
flotery disordered
flour(es) flower(s)
foghte(n) (inf. *fighten*) fought
folwen (inf. *folwen*) follow
folye folly
fomy foam-flecked
foo enemy
foom foam
foond (inf. *finden*) found
footmen men on foot
for for; out of; so that;
  for to to; (ll. 302, 1873)
  for which therefore
forbere (inf. *forberen*) let alone
fordo (inf. *fordon*) destroyed
formes natures

forpined wasting away

forther (l. 1211) *forther moor* further on

forthre(n) help

forthy so, therefore

fortunest (inf. *fortunen*) give good or bad fortune

forward agreement

foryet(e) (inf. *foryeten*) forget

foryeten (inf. *foryeten*) forgotten

foryeve (inf. *foryeven*) forgive

fother cart-load

founden (inf. *finden*) found

foundred (inf. *foundren*) stumbled

fourtenight fortnight

fowel bird

foyne (inf. *foynen*) (l. 1692) let him thrust

foynen (inf. *foynen*) thrust

frakenes freckles

fredom generosity (see Appendix to *An Introduction to Chaucer*)

free noble (see Appendix to *An Introduction to Chaucer*)

freendes friends

freendlich friendly

freeten (inf. *freten*) devoured

frely freely

fressh newly

fressh(e) fresh, gay, bright; (l. 190) brightly

freten devour

fro from

frothen froth

fruit benefit

ful very

fulfild completely full

fulfille (inf. *fulfillen*) satisfy

fully completely; (l. 111) even

furie spirit from hell

fy fie

fyn fine, pure

fyr fire; pyre

gadereth (inf. *gad(e)ren*) gathers

gaf (inf. *given*) gave

gaineth (inf. *gainen*) (l. 318) *us gaineth* helps us; (l. 929) *ther gaineth none obstacles* no obstacles avail; (l. 1897) *him gaineth* there avails him

game joke, entertainment

Galgopheye Gargaphia

gan (inf. *ginnen*) began; often used as an auxiliary to indicate past tense (e.g. *gan knitte* in l. 270, 'knitted')

gardyn garden

gastly ghastly

gaude bright

gayler gaoler

geere behaviour

geery moody, fickle

general (l. 805) universal

gentil noble, magnanimous

gentillesse nobility, mag-nanimity (see Appendix to *An Introduction to Chaucer*)

gere (ll. 158, 1322) equipment

gereful changeable

geres moods

gerland garland

gesse (inf. *gessen*) suppose, conjecture

gete (inf. *getten*) (l. 1897) save

gigginge (inf. *giggen*) fitting straps to

gilt offence

giltelees (l. 454) innocent;
  (l. 457) causelessly
gladen comfort
gladere one who makes glad
gleede burning coal
godhede godhead, divinity
gold-hewen made of gold
goldsmithrye goldsmith's work
gonne (inf. *ginnen*) began (to)
gooldes marigolds
go(o)(n) go, walk; *go sithen*
  see note on l. 663
goon (inf. *goon*) gone
goost spirit
gooth (inf. *goon*) go(es)
goth (inf. *goon*) goes, walks
governaunce order
governour ruler
grace mercy, favour; (l. 734)
  see note
graunte (inf. *graunten*) agree to
graunteth (inf. *graunten*)
  grants
graunting grant
Grece Greece
gree excellence
gre(e)t(e) great; (l. 218) solid
grene green
gretter greater
greves (ll. 637, 783) thickets;
  (l. 649) branches
greveth (inf. *greven*) vexes
grevous severe
grifphon griffin (see note on
  l. 1275)
grisly horrible
groininge discontent
gruccheth (inf. *grucchen*)
  complains
gruf face-down
gye (inf. *gyen*) rule, guide
gyle deception

gypoun vest worn over mail
  and breastplate
gyse custom; fashion; (l. 981)
  at his owene gyse just as he
  chooses
habit dress
habitacioun dwelling-place
hadde (inf. *ha(ve)n*) had,
  should have, would have
haf (inf. *heven*) raised
hakke (inf. *hakken*) cut
han (inf. *ha(ve)n*) have
happed (inf. *happen*) came about
hardinesse daring
hardy daring
haried (inf. *harien*) dragged
  by force
harneys equipment, armour
haubergeoun mail coat
hauberk mail coat
have (inf. *ha(ve)n*) (l. 1856)
  preserve
heed head; *(up)on his heed*
  on pain of death; *by myn
  heed* I swear
heeld (inf. *holden*) kept
heele wellbeing
heeled (inf. *heelen*) cured
heer hair
heer-agains against this
heerbiforn before this
heer(e) here
he(e)re (inf. *he(e)ren*) hear
he(e)ris hair
heete (inf. *hoten*) promises
heigh(e) high, great, serious,
  noble
helmes helmets
helpeth (inf. *helpen*) (l. 1962)
  what helpeth it? what is the
  use (of)?
hem them

hemself themselves
henne away
hente(n) (inf. *henten*) seize(d), caught
heraud(es) herald(s)
herd (adj.) (l. 1660) *the thikke herd*, the one with thick hair
herde (inf. *he(e)ren*) heard
her(e) her
Hereos lovesickness (see note on ll. 511–18)
helden (*with*) (inf. *holden*) (l. 1659) supported
herknen listen to
herkneth (inf. *herknen*) listen
hert hart
herte heart
herte-spoon pit of the stomach
heste command
hevenisshly divinely
hevinesse grief
hewe (noun) complexion, colour
hewe (inf. *hewen*) chop
hider (to) here
hidouse terrifying
hidously terribly
hie (inf. *hien*) hasten
highte (noun) *on highte* (l. 926) aloud, (l. 1749) in the air; (l. 2061) *maked upon highte* built up
hight(e) (inf. *hoten*) was (were) called, be called; (l. 1614) promised
himselven himself
hir(e) her; their
his his; its
holde(n) (inf. *holden*) (l. 449) obliged; (l. 648) make; (l. 832) followed; (l. 1861) considered to be

holdeth (inf. *holden*) (l. 1010) consider
holm holm-oak
holwe sunken
hond hand; (l. 745) *of myn hond* at my hands
honestly suitably
honge(th) (inf. *hangen*) hang(s), hung
hoo! stop!
hool whole
hoolly completely
hoom home
hoost army
hoot(e) (adj.) hot, fervent; (l. 951) *this hoote fare* these heated goings on; (l. 953) *hoot and cold* see note
hoote (adv.) (l. 879) fervently
hoppesteres dancing
hostelries lodgings
hou how; *hou...that* however
houndes dogs
housbondes husbands
humblesse humility
hunte huntsman
hunteresse huntress
hurtleth (inf. *hurtlen*) hurls
hust hushed
hye (adj.) high
hye (noun) (l. 2121) haste
imaginacioun fantasy
imagining conception
in (noun) lodging
Inde India
infortune ill-fortune
iniquitee wickedness
inned lodged
ire anger
iren iron

jalous(e) jealous
jalousie jealousy
japed (inf. *japen*) tricked
joinant adjoining
jolitee fun
journee day's journey
Jove Jupiter
juge judge
Julius Julius Caesar
Juno Juno
juste(n) (inf. *justen*) joust
justes jousting match
juwise sentence
kan (inf. *konnen*) can;
   know(s) how to; (l. 922)
   recognizes; (ll. 950, 2206)
   shows
kaytyf wretched
keep (l. 531) *took keep*
   observed
kembd (inf. *kemben*) combed
kempe coarse
kene sharp
kepe (inf. *kepen*) (ll. 1380,
   2102) care; (l. 2471) guard
kepere guardian
kervere carver
kerving sculpture
kinde (l. 1593) nature;
   (l. 543) *al in another kinde*
   completely transformed.
   See Appendix to *An*
   Introduction to Chaucer
kindrede kindred
kist (inf. *kissen*) kissed
knarry gnarled
knaves servants
knew (inf. *knowen*) (ll. 739,
   790) recognized
knighthod (l. 1245) *knighthod*
   of hir hond their skill in
   war

knowe (inf. *knowen*) known
knyf knife
korven (inf. *kerven*) cut
koude (inf. *konnen*) could;
   knew how to
kouthe (inf. *konnen*) could
la(a)s snare
lacerte muscle
lacinge (inf. *lacen*) fastening
lad(de) (inf. *leden*) led
laft (inf. *leven*) left
large large, broad, wide;
   at thy (his) large at liberty
largely fully
las see *laas*
lasse and moore see note on
   l. 898
lat (inf. *leten*) let
launde field
laurer laurel
lay (inf. *lyen*) (l. 112) camped
layneres straps
lechecraft medical skill
leef (noun) leaf
leef (inf. *leven*) leave
leep (inf. *lepen*) leapt
leeste least, slightest
leet (inf. *leten*) let, allowed,
   caused
leeve dear
leeveth (inf. *le(e)ven*) believe
lefte (inf. *leven*) left, gave up
lene (adj.) lean
lene (inf. *lenen*) give
lenger longer
leo(u)n lion
lese (inf. *lesen*) lose
lesinge losing
lesinges lies
lest pleasure
leste see *liste*
lete (inf. *leten*) leave

letted (inf. *letten*) prevented

letten hinder; (l. 459) *letten of* refrain from

leve leave

ley (inf. *leyen*) (l. 1700) *ley on* attack

leyde (inf. *leyen*) (!. 526) *him leyde* lay

leye (inf. *leyen*) lay

leyser leisure

lief pleasing

lif see *lyf*

lifly in a life-like way

liggen lie

ligginge (inf. *liggen*) lying

lighte bright, shining

lightly cheerful(ly)

ligne descent

liketh (inf. *liken*) it pleases

liknesse simile(s)

linage family, descent

linde lime

list it pleases (e.g. *me list* or *list me* I like, I desire)

liste, leste it pleased (e.g. *him leste* it pleased him, he liked; *as hire liste* as she pleased)

listes tilting-ground

lite(l) small, little

lith (inf. *lyen*) lies

lives alive

lo behold (see note on l. 933)

lode load

lond land

long long, tall

longen be appropriate

longes lungs

longeth (inf. *longen*) belongs, is appropriate

loode-sterre pole-star

looking glance

looth see note on l. 979

lordshipe sovereignty; (l. 969) protection

lowe humbly

Lucina Lucina (see note on ll. 1217–28)

lust joy; desire(s)

lustily joyfully

lustinesse joy

lusty joyful, rigorous

lyche-wake watch over a corpse

lyf, lif life

Lygurge Lycurgus

lyk like

lymes limbs

maad (inf. *maken*) made

maat downcast

maide virgin

maidenhede virginity

maintaine (l. 583) maintain; (l. 920) stand by

maister (l. 2044) *maister strete* main street

maistow mayst thou

maked (inf. *maken*) made, caused

maketh (inf. *maken*) (l. 2177) causes

malencolik melancholic

manace threat

manasinge threatening

maner(e) way; (l. 1017) *every maner* every kind of; (l. 1031) *in manere of* like

manhede courage

manie mania

manly courageously

mansioun dwelling (but see note on l. 1116)

mantelet short cloak

mapul maple

marbul marble

Mars, Marte Mars

martireth (inf. *martiren*) martyrs, punishes

matrimoigne matrimony

maugree despite; (ll. 311, 1760) *maugree his heed* despite all he can do; (l. 749) *maugree al thy might* despite all you can do; (l. 938) *maugree hir eyen two* despite all they can do

mayst mayst; art capable

maystow mayst thou

Medea Medea

meeste, and leeste highest and lowest

meete properly

meeth mead

Meleagre Meleager

memorie (l. 1840) *in memorie* conscious

men men, people; one

mencioun mention

mene (inf. *menen*) mean, intend; say

mente (inf. *menen*) intended

Mercurie Mercury

meschaunce misfortune

mescheef harm

meschief disadvantage

messager messenger

mester occupation

mete (adj.) fit

mete (noun) food

meynee servants

might power; (l. 1254) *hath his might* is in possession of his full strength

ministre executor

minour miner

mirour mirror

mirre myrrh

misboden (inf. *misboden*) ill-treated

misfille (inf. *misfallen*) it went amiss

mishappe (inf. *mishappen*) it goes badly (for)

mo more

mone lamentation

montance value

mood anger

moore more, greater; (l. 683) *withouten any moore* without more delay; (l. 1458) *withoute moore* as my only request

moost most

mooste greatest

moot (no inf.) must

mordre murder

mordringe murder

morwe(ninge) morning

mosel muzzle

moste must

mowe may

muche (l. 2029) *in as muche as* in order that

muchel much

murie cheerful, pleasant

murmure complaint, dissatisfaction

myn my, mine

myrie see *murie*

myster (l. 852) *what myster men* what kind of men

nailes claws

nailinge see note on l. 1645

nakers kettle-drums

nam (inf. *been*) am not

name name, reputation

namely especially

namo no others
namoore no more
Narcisus Narcissus
nas (inf. *been*) was not
nat not
nathelees nevertheless
naught not
nay no
ne neither, nor, not
necligence negligence
nedes necessarily; (l. 619)
  nedes cost necessarily
nedeth is (are) necessary
neer nearer
nekke neck
ner see *fer*
nercotikes narcotics
nere (inf. *been*) were not,
  would not be, was not
Nero Nero
newe newly
nexte nearest
nis (inf. *been*) (there) is not
no thing not at all
noght not
nolde (inf. *willen*) would not
nombre number
none no
nones for the nones (l. 21)
  particularly; (l. 565) indeed
noon no, none
noot (inf. *witen*) do not know
norisshinge period of growth
ny nearly; *wel ny* very nearly
obeisaunce obedience
obsequies funeral ceremonies
observaunce (ll. 187, 642,
  1406) rite; (l. 458) duty
of of; off
offence injury
offende(d) (inf. *offenden*)
  injure(d)

offensioun hurt
office (l. 2005) rite; (l. 560)
  fil in office got a position
officere official
ofte often; (l. 454) *ofte
  times* frequently; (l. 498)
  ofte a day many times a day
okes oaks
on on, in
ones once; (l. 1530) *ones on a
  time* on one occasion
Oo! listen!
ook oak
oold old
o(o)(n) one; (l. 913) *evere in
  oon* continually; (l. 923)
  after oon alike; (l. 979)
  that oon one; (l. 1260)
  many on many; (l. 1715)
  of oon and oother in pairs
oonly only, merely
ooth oath
oother other, the other,
  another
opie opium
opinio(u)n belief; (l. 622)
  intention; (l. 1269) choice
ordeyned (inf. *ordeynen*)
  provided
ordina(u)nce (l. 2154) decree;
  by ordinance in procession
ordre (l. 1076) *by ordre* in
  order
orison prayer
othes oaths
ought at all
out (l. 765) *out of* lacking in
outhees outcry
outher either
outrely outright
over over, beyond; *over al*
  everywhere, anywhere

overriden (inf. *overriden*) run
  over
overthwart across
owene own
pace (inf. *pacen*) pass
pacience patience
paleys palace
palfreys saddle-horses
pan head
paramour(s) (l. 297) as a man
  loves a woman; (l. 1254)
  devotedly
pardee indeed
parementz rich mantles
parfit perfect
parlement (l. 448) decree;
  (l. 2112) assembly
part share; side; (l. 1934)
  have...part (of) protect;
  (l. 1966) *the moore part*
  the most part
partie (l. 1799) prejudiced
  judge
party mixed
pas foot, feet; *a pas* at walking
  pace
passant pre-eminent
passeth (inf. *passen*) continues
passinge (inf. *passen*) surpassing
payen pagan
pees peace
penaunce suffering
pencel artist's brush
Penneus Peneus
pennon small pointed flag
peple people
perfit perfect
Perotheus Pirithous
perrye jewellery
perturben disturb
peyne pain, torture
peynted (inf. *peynten*) painted

phisik medical treatment
pighte (inf. *pichen*) (l. 1831)
  pighte him fell
piler pillar
pilours pillagers
pine (inf. *pinen*) torture
pine (noun) suffering
pipen (in) blow (on)
pipes pipes; (l. 1894) veins
pitee pity
pitous (l. 95) full of pity;
  (ll. 972, 1061) pitiful
pitously pitifully
place (l. 1541) field
plain see *pleyn*
plat plain
plates see note on l. 1263
plesaunce pleasure, will
pley joke, game
pleye (inf. *pleyen*) joke,
  amuse (oneself)
pleyinge amusement
pleyn, plain (l. 629) full;
  (l. 606) fully; (l. 1603)
  severe; (l. 130) *pleyn
  bataille* open battle; (l. 233)
  short and plain long and
  short of it
pleyne(n) (on) lament, complain (about)
pleynly plainly, openly
Pluto Pluto
point (l. 643) object; (l. 1908)
  part
polax battle axe
pomel top
porter gatekeeper
portreiture(s) painting(s)
portreyinge painting
portreyour painter
pose (inf. *posen*) (l. 304)
  I pose let us suppose

positif (l. 309) *positif lawe* human law

povre poor

povrely poorly, in poverty, humbly

pray(e) prey

preesseth (inf. *pre(e)ssen*) crowd

preeved (inf. *preven*) proved

prescience foreknowledge

preyde (inf. *preyen*) begged

preye (inf. *preyen*) pray, beg

preyere prayer, supplication

priketh (inf. *priken*) urges, dashes

prikinge (inf. *priken*) rushing, riding

prikke stab

prime early morning

pris reputation

privee secret

prively secretly

privetee secret

profreth (inf. *profren*) offers

progressiouns see note on l. 2155

proprely (l. 1929) exactly

proudly (l. 294) haughtily

Pruce Prussian

Puella see note on l. 1187

pure very

purveiaunce providence

putte (inf. *putten*) put; (l. 2084) *putte in* thrust in

pykepurs pickpocket

pyne suffering

qualm plague

questioun discussion

queynt(e) (inf. *quenchen*) (ll. 1463, 1478) quenched; (ll. 1476, 1479) was extinguished

queynte (adj.) strange

quiked (inf. *quiken*) revived

quite (inf. *quiten*) ransom

quitly completely

quod (inf. *quethen*) said

quook (inf. *quaken*) trembled

quyke alive

rad (inf. *reden*) read over

rage (l. 1127) raging wind

ran (inf. *runnen*) (l. 544) *ran him in his minde* suddenly occurred to him

rancour ill-feeling

ransake (inf. *ransaken*) search

rasour razor

rather sooner

raughte (inf. *rechen*) reached

raunsoun ransom

rebelling rebellion

recche(th) (inf. *recchen*) care(s)

reconforte (inf. *reconforten*) (l. 1994) *hem reconforte* take new heart

recorde (inf. *recorden*) confirm

rede (adj.) red

rede (inf. *reden*) advise

redily in readiness

redoutinge reverence

redy ready

reed (help) for it

refuge shelter

regioun kingdom; (l. 1899) area of the body

registre contents of book (see note on l. 1954)

regne (ll. 8, 1441) realm; (l. 766) rule

rehersing repetition

rek(e)ne(d) (inf. *reknen*) list(ed)

remedie way out

remenant remainder

renges ranks

renne(th) (inf. *rennen*) run(s), flow(s)

renoun reputation

rente (noun) income

rente (inf. *renden*) tore

rentinge (inf. *renden*) tearing

repplicacioun answering back

rescus rescue, attempt

rese (inf. *resen*) shake

resoun reason

resouneth (inf. *resounen*) resounds

respit delay

retenue see note on ll. 1643–5

retourninge return

reuled (inf. *reulen*) governed

rewe (noun) row

rewe (inf. *rewen*) have pity

rewefulleste most sorrowful

reyneth (inf. *reynen*) rains

richesse wealth

right (adv.) just, very, quite, directly

right (noun) (l. 2231) justice

righte (adj.) direct

rightes (ll. 994, 1242) *at alle rightes* in every respect

ringes ringlets

rit (inf. *riden*) ride(s)

rite religious ceremony

roially in royal state

romed (inf. *romen*) roamed

romen roam

ronnen (inf. *rennen*) ran

rood (inf. *riden*) rode

roos (inf. *risen*) rose

roreth (inf. *roren*) (l. 2023) *roreth of* resounds with

rouketh (inf. *rouken*) cowers

route company

routhe (a) pity

Rubeus see note on l. 1187

ruggy rough

ruine collapse

rumbel rumbling

sad composed

sadel-bowe projection at front of saddle

sadly firmly

Salomon Solomon

salueth (inf. *saluen*) greets

saluing greeting

salves ointments

Sampsoun Samson

sanguin blood-red

sarge serge (see note on l. 1710)

Saturne, Saturnus Saturn

saugh (inf. *seen*) saw

save (conj.) except for

save (noun) sage

savinge except

sawe saying; (l. 668) *al his sawe* everything he said

sayn, sey(e)n say

scapen escape

Scithia Scythia, a district north of the Black Sea

scriptures learned writings

see (noun) sea

seege siege

se(en) see

seene (l. 66) apparent

seet (inf. *sitten*) sat

seide see *seyde*

seigh (inf. *seen*) saw

seinte holy

seistow (inf. *seyn*) saist thou

seith (inf. *seyn*) says

selde seldom

selve same

semed (inf. *semen*) (l. 2112) *semed me* it would appear

semely fitting

sene (adj.) (l. 1440) visible

sene (verb) see

sentence decision, opinion

sepulture funeral rites

sermoning discussion

servage servitude

servise service; (ll. 568, 577) position

serye argument

seso(u)n season

seten (inf. *sitten*) sat, remained

sette (inf. *sitten*) (l. 712) reckon; (l. 2126) fixed; (l. 683) *sette him doun* sat down

seurete pledge

seyde(n), *seide(n)* (inf. *sayn*, *sey(e)n*) said

seyen see *sayn*

seye(th) (inf. *sayn*, *sey(e)n*) say

seyn (inf. *seen*) seen; (l. 807) *seyn biforn* foreseen

shaft stick, spear

shal (inf. *shullen*) shall be; (ll. 1420, 1466) must; (l. 1696) shall go; (ll. 1847, 1848) would

shaltou shalt thou

shamefast modest

shap (l. 1058) form

shape(n) (inf. *shapen*) contrived, fixed, destined; (l. 1683) arrange

sharp fierce

she(e)ne beautiful, shining

shent (inf. *shenden*) injured

shepne stable

shere scissors

sherte shirt

shet (inf. *shetten*) shut

shewed (inf. *shewen*) declared

shiveren (inf. *shiveren*) splinter

shode crown of the head

sholde (inf. *shullen*) should, would; (l. 1630) must

sholdest (inf. *shullen*) shouldst

shoon (inf. *shinen*) shone

shortly briefly, in a short time

shot missile

shrighte (inf. *shryken*) shrieked

shul(len) shall

shuldres shoulders

shynes shins

sighte sight; (l. 814) Providence

sike(d) (inf. *siken*) sigh(e)d

siker certain; *siker of* secure in

sikerly truly, certainly

sikes sighs

sin since

sit (inf. *sitten*) (ll. 749, 942) dwells

sith(en) since

sithe (l. 1019) *often sithe* often

slakke slow

sle (inf. *sleen*) kill

sleen kill

sleep (inf. *slepen*) slept

sleere killer

sleeth (inf. *sleen*) kills, slays

sleighte cunning

slep(es) sleep(s)

slepy sleep-producing

slider slippery

slogardie laziness

slough, slow (inf. *sleen*) slew, killed

slyly discreetly

smerte (adj.) stinging, piercing

smerte (inf. *smerten*) (l. 536)
  me smerte it hurts me

smite(th) (inf. *smiten*) strike(s)

smokinge (inf. *smoken*)
  burning incense in

smoot (inf. *smiten*) struck

so (l. 1379) provided that;
  (l. 1389) *so that* so long as

socour assistance

sodeynliche, sodeynly suddenly

softe gently, quietly

solempnitee ceremony, festivity

som some; one; (l. 1903) *this
  al and som* this is the long
  and short of it

somdel somewhat

somer summer

sone son

song (inf. *singen*) sang

songe(n) (inf. *singen*) sung

so(o)ng (inf. *singen*) sang

soor(e) (adj.) aching; (l. 1946)
  wounded

soore (adv.) severe(ly),
  extremely, passionately

soor(e) (noun) pain

sooth(ly) truly

soper supper

sore severely

sorwe sorrow

sorweful sorrowful

sorwen (inf. *sorwen*) are
  miserable

sorweth (inf. *sorwen*) is
  miserable

sory wretched

sothe for sothe truly

soun(es) sounds

soutil (l. 1172) fine; (l. 1191)
  skilful

soverein principal

space space of time

spak (inf. *speken*) spoke

spare (inf. *sparen*) refrain,
  give up

sparre beam

sparth battle-axe

speces kinds, qualities

special (l. 159) *in special*
  distinctly

spedde (inf. *speden*) (l. 359)
  him spedde hurried

spede (inf. *speden*) (l. 1700)
  God spede you good luck
  to you

speke (inf. *speken*) speak;
  (ll. 971, 1245) *(as for) to
  speke of* in respect of

spere spear

spicerye mixture of spices

spores spurs

sprad(de) (inf. *spreden*) spread

springe (inf. *springen*) (l. 1633)
  break; (l. 1664) rise

spronge (inf. *springen*) sprung
  up

square strong

squier(es) squire(s)

stable unchanging

stablissed (inf. *stablissen*)
  established

Stace Statius

stake see note on l. 1694

starf (inf. *sterven*) died

startlinge leaping

statue image

staves sticks

steede(s) war-horses

stent(e) (inf. *stenten*) stop(ped)

stenten cease

sterres stars

stert spring

sterte, stirte (inf. *sterten*)
  leapt; (l. 186) spring up;
  (ll. 535, 1826) sprang up;
  (l. 904) started
sterve die
stevene time; voice
stierne grim
stille quietly
stirte see *sterte*
stith anvil
stok family
stoke (inf. *stoken*) stab
stole (inf. *stelen*) stolen
stomblen (inf. *stomblen*)
  stumble
stonden stands; (l. 315)
  stonden in hir grace receive
  her favour; (l. 464) occur
stondeth (inf. *stonden*) stands
stongen (inf. *stingen*) sting
stoon stone
stounde moment; (l. 354) *oo*
  stounde for a single
  moment
stoute strong
straughte (inf. *strechen*)
  stretched
stree straw
streight(e) directly
streit narrow
strepe (inf. *strepen*) strip
strif strife, argument
stronge strong, severe
stroof (inf. *striven*) vied
strook blow
stubbes stumps
studie fit of meditation
stynten put a stop to
stynt(e)(th) (inf. *stynten*)
  cease(d) (talking); put an
  end to
subtil intricate

successiouns by successiouns
  in succession to one
  another
suffisaunt adequate
suffised (inf. *suffisen*) sufficed
suffiseth (inf. *suffisen*) (it) is
  (are) enough
suffren (l. 87) permit
suite (l. 2015) *of the same*
  suite to match
sustene (inf. *sustene*) hold
  up
suster sister(-in-law)
sustren sisters
swelte (inf. *swelten*) fainted
swerd(es) sword(s)
swich such (a)
swoor (inf. *sweren*) swore
swoote sweet
sworen (inf. *sweren*) promised
swough murmuring (of wind)
swowned (inf. *swownen*)
  fainted
swowninge (inf. *swownen*)
  fainting
syk sick
taak (inf. *taken*) take; (l. 226)
  endure
taas heap
table tablet
take(n) (inf. *taken*) taken;
  (ll. 1008, 1693, 1750) taken
  prisoner, captured
tare seed
targe light shield
tarien (l. 2962) *tarien forth*
  the day spend the whole
  day
Tars Turkestan
teene annoyance
teeres, teeris tears
telleth (inf. *tellen*) tell

Glossary

terme duration

termes periods

testeres head-pieces

thank gratitude

thankes his (hir) thankes willingly, gladly

than(ne) then

that that; so that; when

ther there; where; *ther as* whereas, where

ther-biforn beforehand

therto moreover

therwithal thereupon

Theseus Theseus

thider to there, to it

thiderwards towards there, towards it

thikke (l. 198) solid; (l. 1652) densely; *thikke of* (l. 217) thick with

thilke the same, that

thinges (l. 1485) rites

thinketh (inf. *thinken*) (l. 1009) it seems (see note)

thirled (inf. *thirlen*) pierced

thise these

tho (adv.) then

tho (pron.) those

thonked (inf. *thonken*) thanked

though though; (l. 1096) yet

thoughte (inf. *thinken*) (it) seemed (e.g. *him thoughte* it seemed to him)

thral enslaved

threed thread

threste (inf. *thresten*) push

thridde third

thries thrice

thurgh through; out of; because of

thurghfare passage

thurgh-girt pierced through

thurghout right through

thyn thy, thine

thyselven thyself

til to; *til that* (l. 286) until

time (l. 1717) *by time* early

tirannye tyranny, arbitrary attitude

tiraunt tyrant

to to; for; too

tobreste (inf. *tobresten*) break to pieces

tobrosten (inf. *tobrosten*) shattered

togidre together

tohewen (inf. *tohewen*) cut to pieces

tolde see *toold*

tomorwe tomorrow

tonge tongue, speech

tonne-greet wide as a barrel

too toe

took (inf. *taken*) (l. 1408) understood

toold, tolde (inf. *tellen*) said, told, recounted

torn (l. 162) dragged

toshrede (inf. *toshreden*) cut to shreds

tour tower

touret turret

to(u)rneyinge (inf. *tourneyen*) tournament

tourrettes swivel-rings (for attaching leads)

Trace Thrace

trais traces

transfigure (inf. *transfiguren*) (reflexive) appear in another form

transmutacioun changeability

trapped having trappings

Glossary

trappures horse-trappings
travaille labour
travaillinge in labour
treso(u)n treachery
trespas offence
tretee negotiation
trewe true, faithful
trewely faithfully, indeed
trompe(s) trumpet(s)
trompours trumpeters
tronchoun broken shaft of spear
trone throne
trouthe promise, word; (l. 1951) fidelity
trowed (inf. *trowen*) believe(d)
Troye Troy
Turkeys Turkish
turneying see *tourneyinge*
Turnus Turnus
tweye two
unknowe unknown
unkonninge ignorant
unkouth curious
unset unappointed
unto (l. 1690) against; (l. 1860) for
untressed (inf. *untressen*) let down
unwist of unknown to
unyolden without surrendering
up up; (l. 849) on
upright face upwards
upriste uprising
usage practice
usedest (inf. *usen*) enjoyed
vale valley
vassellage prowess
veine-blod blood-letting
venerye hunting
ventusing cupping

venym poison
verraily truly
verray true
vertu (l. 578) excellence; (l. 1391) power; (ll. 1891, 1892) see note
vestimentz vestments
veyn(e) empty, vain
veze blast
vileynye (ll. 84, 1871) dishonour (see Appendix to *An Introduction to Chaucer*)
voiden discharge
vois voice
vomit emetic
Vulcanus Vulcan
waiteth (inf. *waiten*) watches
wake-pleyes funeral games
wan (adj.) gloomy (see note on l. 1598)
wan (inf. *winnen*) won, conquered
wane (inf. *wanen*) decline
wanhope despair
wantinge lacking
wanye (inf. *wanien*) (l. 1220) (of moon) wane
war (ll. 38, 840) *was war* noticed; (l. 360) *be war* be careful
waste devastated
wasted (inf. *wasten*) decayed
wasteth (inf. *wasten*) decays
wawes waves
wayke weak
waymentinge lamentation
wedde (l. 360) *lith to wedde* is at stake
wedden marry
wede clothing
weel (adj.) (l. 68) prosperous; (l. 968) see *faire*

216

we(e)l(e) well; very; certainly;
(l. 1251) *wel was him* he
was lucky; (l. 2185) *take it
weel* accept cheerfully

weep (inf. *wepen*) wept

wele (l. 37) success; (l. 414)
happiness; (l. 1815) *in hir
wele* at their happiest

welle source

wende (inf. *wenden*) go,
vanish

wende (inf. *wenen*)
believed

wene(n) (inf. *wenen*) suppose

wepe (inf. *wepen*) weep

wep(e)ne weapon

were (inf. *been*) were, would
be

were (inf. *weren*) (l. 2090)
wear

were (inf. *weren*) defend

wered(e) (inf. *weren*) wore

weren (inf. *been*) were, had
been

werre war

werreye(n) make war (on)

wessh (inf. *wasshen*) washed

wete wet

wex (inf. *waxen*) grew

wexeth (inf. *waxen*) becomes

wexinge (of moon) waxing

wey(e) road, way

weyeth (inf. *weyen*) weighs

weylaway alas

whan when

what what; why; who; *what
so* whatever; *what for*
what with

wheither (l. 267) which (of
two); (l. 997) whichever;
(l. 998) whether

whelp cub

wher(e) (ll. 243, 1394, 1539)
whether

which which; who; *which a*
what a

whil while

whilom formerly

whippeltree dogwood

whit white

wight person

wighte weight

wikke evil

wilnen desire

wilnest (inf. *wilnen*) desirest

wilneth (inf. *wilnen*) desires

wilugh willow

wise manner; (l. 480) *double
wise* twofold

wis(ly) certainly, surely

wiste (inf. *witen*) knew

wit mind

witen know

withoute(n) without; (l. 1050)
on the outside

withseyn deny

witing knowledge

wo misery, sorrow, harm;
(l. 42) lamentation

wode(s) wood(s)

wodebinde honeysuckle

wofuller more unhappy

wolde would

woldestow (inf. *willen*) wouldst
thou

wol(e) will, intend to

wolt (inf. *willen*) wilt,
desirest

woltow (inf. *willen*) wilt thou

wommanhede womanliness

wonder (adj.) wonderful

wonder (adv.) incredibly,
extremely

wone custom

woneden (inf. *wonen*) (had) dwelt

wonne (inf. *winnen*) conquered

wont accustomed

wood mad, enraged

woodly fiercely

woodnesse madness

wook (inf. *waken*) woke

woost (inf. *witen*) knowest

woot (inf. *witen*) knows

worshipe honour, worship

worshipful honourable

worthily suitably

worthinesse nobility

worthy noble; (ll. 973, 1522, 1936) worthy

wostow (inf. *witen*) dost thou know

wowke week

wrastleth (inf. *wrastlen*) wrestle

wrecched wretched

wreke (inf. *wreken*) avenge

wrethe wreath

wroghte (inf. *werchen*) fashioned, made; caused; done; created

wrothe angry, enraged

wyf wife

wykes weeks

wyn wine

wys prudent, skilful

wyve (l. 1002) *to wyve* as a wife

yaf (inf. *yeven*) gave

ybete embroidered, beaten

yborn born, carried

ybounde(n) (inf. *binden*) (l. 291) obliged; (l. 1293) bound

ybrent (inf. *brennen*) burnt

ybro(u)ght (inf. *bringen*) brought

yburied (inf. *burien*) buried

yclenched clamped

ycleped (inf. *clepen*) called

yclothed (inf. *clothen*) dressed

ycorve (inf. *carven*) cut

ydo(n) (inf. *do(o)n*) done, acted, taken

ydrawe (inf. *drawen*) dragged

ydriven (inf. *driven*) driven

ydropped (inf. *droppen*) sprinkled

ye you

ye (ll. 238, 1822) eye; *at ye* at a glance

ye(e)r year, years

yelewe yellow

yelpe (inf. *yelpen*) boast

yemen attendants

yerde yard; (l. 529) staff

yere year

yet yet, still; (l. 1159) moreover

yeve (inf. *yeven*) give

yeve(n) see *yiven*

yeveth (inf. *yeven*) gives

yfetered (inf. *feteren*) fettered

yground (inf. *grinden*) ground, sharpened

yholde (inf. *holden*) considered as

yhurt (inf. *hurten*) wounded

yif (inf. *yiven*) give

yiftes gifts

yive (inf. *yiven*) give

yiven, yeven (inf. *yiven*) given

ylaft (inf. *leven*) left

yliche alike

ylike like, alike, equally

ymaked (inf. *maken*) made (into); held

ymet (inf. *meten*) met (in battle)
ymeynd mingled
ynough enough
yolden (inf. *yelden*) *up yolden* given up
yond over there
yonge young
yore (l. 955) *yore agon* long ago
youling howling
yow you
ypayed (inf. *payen*) paid
Ypolita Hippolyta
yraft (inf. *reven*) snatched away
yronne (inf. *rennen*) arranged
yronnen (inf. *rennen*) run together

ysaid (inf. *say(e)n*) said
yscalded (inf. *scalden*) scalded
ysent (inf. *senden*) sent
yserved (inf. *serven*) treated
yset (inf. *setten*) appointed
yslain (inf. *sleen*) slain
yslawe (inf. *sleen*) slain
yspoken (inf. *speken*) proposed
yspreynd scattered
ystiken (inf. *stiken*) stabbed
ystorve (inf. *sterven*) killed
ysworn (inf. *sweren*) sworn
yturned (inf. *turnen*) (l. 380) cast; (l. 1204) transformed
yvele hardly
ywedded (inf. *wedden*) married
ywonne (inf. *winnen*) won
ywrye (inf. *wryen*) covered